BAWA STAIRCASES

A **TALISMAN BOOK** FOR LAURENCE KING

First published in 2019

Talisman Publishing Pte Ltd
talisman@apdsing.com
www.talismanpublishing.com
ISBN: 978-981-11-8574-8

Laurence King Publishing Ltd
enquiries@laurenceking.com
www.laurenceking.com
ISBN: 978-178-62-7430-4

Text © David Robson
Photography © Sebastian Posingis
Editor Kim Inglis
Copy Editor Paul Haines
Designers Norreha Sayuti, Stephy Chee
Studio Manager Janice Ng
Publisher Ian Pringle

A catalogue record for this book is available from the British Library

Printed in Singapore

BAWA STAIRCASES

DAVID ROBSON

PHOTOGRAPHY **SEBASTIAN POSINGIS**

CONTENTS

Part I　　**Introduction**

10　Preface

14　Towards Architecture

18　Staircases of the Italian Renaissance

40　Staircases of the German Baroque — Balthasar Neumann

48　Sri Lanka's Architectural Heritage

Part II　　**Bawa's Built Projects**

76　Bawa's Staircases in Sri Lanka

78　Lunuganga

88　The Deraniyagala House

90　St Thomas's Prep School

92　Tennis Club

94　The A S H de Silva House

96　The Ena de Silva House

100　The Raffel House

102　St Bridget's Montessori School

104　The Polontalawa Estate Bungalow

106　Geoffrey Bawa's Town House

110　Steel Corporation Tower

111　Steel Corporation Offices

112　Tourist Village and Railway Station

114　The Beach Hotel

118　The Serendib Hotel

120　The Neptune Hotel

122　The State Mortgage Bank

124　The Martenstyn House

126　House for Lidia Duchini

128　Mohoti Walaawe

130　Institute of Integral Education

134　Triton Hotel

136　New Sri Lanka Parliament

140　Ruhunu University Campus

146　House for Sunethra Bandaranaike

148　Fitzherbert House

152　Chloe de Soysa House

154　Kandalama Hotel

158　Jayakody House

160　Lighthouse Hotel

166　Blue Water Hotel

170　The David Spenser House

172　The Jayawardene House

174　Glossary, Bibliography, Photo Credits, Acknowledgments

Preface

Stairs fulfil the simple practical function of facilitating movement from one level to another. Within buildings they provide access between successive floors, while outside them they reduce awkward slopes to a series of manageable steps. They accommodate bipedal movement, offering a quicker and more compact alternative to ramps and a safer and gentler alternative to ladders.

The 'pitch' of a staircase is determined by the ratio of the vertical 'rise' of each step to its horizontal 'going'. Different pitches are deemed to be suitable for different functions. Thus, a steeper pitch might be used in a dwelling where there are fewer people and less available space, while a gentler pitch might be used in a public building serving large numbers of people. The smallest 'going' must be wide enough to accommodate the ball of the foot and the highest 'rise' should not overly tax the muscles.

Comfort dictates that as 'goings' increase so 'rises' should decrease. One rule of thumb used by architects lays down that the sum of twice the 'rise' plus the 'going' in centimetres should equal 65. Thus, a domestic staircase with 'goings' of 25 centimetres might have 'rises' of 20 centimetres, while a public stair with 'goings' of 35 centimetres might have 'rises' of 15 centimetres.

But staircases do so much more than simply enable us to change level. They combine horizontal and vertical movement, offering ever changing vistas, and are potentially the most dynamic and theatrical spatial elements of a building. And they are often imbued with arcane religious or cultural significance.

In the past, some staircases were made deliberately steep in order to cause discomfort and instil awe. Thus, the staircase that climbs up to the palace citadel at Yapahuva in Sri Lanka rises at an angle of more than 45 degrees in order to force visitors into a posture of obeisance.

In Delhi, the Mogul emperor Humayun died after falling down his library staircase and striking his head on a stone step. When his widow constructed a magnificent garden tomb in his memory, the staircase up to the main platform was constructed with an exaggerated pitch in order to remind visitors of the cause of his death.

Shallow staircases were used when ceremonial pomp was called for. The staircase in the Residenz at Würzburg was sufficiently shallow to enable the Prince Bishop to progress up it in state, or even to be carried up in a palanquin. It functioned as a key space within a grand *promenade architecturale* that linked the ground-floor *porte-cochère* with the White Hall and Imperial Hall above.

During the 19th century, opera houses were built as much to create a stage for the audience as for the performers. Thus, the Paris Opera by Charles Garnier incorporated vast swirling staircases in its foyer to serve as a monumental showpiece, enabling women in elaborate gowns to ascend and descend in great style.

Staircases have always figured prominently in the architecture of Sri Lanka. This is in no small part due to the fact that it is a mountainous country with a rocky, boulder strewn landscape. Early settlements grew up in the shallow river valleys of the northern plains, where the valley floors were exploited for agriculture. Villages, temples and monasteries were established on higher sloping ground and stairs; built up of stone or cut into naked rock, they became an integral part of the man-made landscape.

Some of the oldest surviving examples are found cut into outcrops of naked rock in ancient monasteries, such as that at Vessagiriya on the edge of Anuradhapura which dates originally

PAGES 2/3: Staircase in Geoffrey Bawa's Colombo home.

PAGE 4: Stairs leading up to the South Terrace, Lunuganga.

PREVIOUS PAGE: Main staircase, Mihintale.

OPPOSITE: The top flight and portal of the staircase at Yapahuwa.

from the second half of the 1st Millennium BC. Later, during the great Anuradhapura period that spanned the whole of the 1st Millennium AD, elaborate staircases were incorporated into temples, monastic buildings and palaces.

Sri Lankan architect Geoffrey Bawa came late to his chosen career having first studied to become a lawyer. His interest in staircases can be traced back to the time when he enrolled to study architecture at the Architectural Association in London during the mid-1950s and in particular to his final study year, spanning late 1956 and early 1957, which he spent in Rome. During that year he wrote a dissertation on the work of the German Baroque architect, Balthasar Neumann.

We know, from his dissertation and from recalled conversations, that during that year, as well as visiting Neumann's buildings in Bavaria, he visited and studied the staircases of Bernini and Borromini in Rome as well as those of Vignola at Caprarola and Bagnaia. In his dissertation he connects Neumann back to Rome and to the work of Baroque architects such as Bernini and Borromini:

Neumann's palace designs go back to the joint work of Bernini and Borromini in the Barberini Palace in Rome. In the junctions and reflections of spaces and in the handling of staircases, many of the great architects of the period owe a debt to Bernini.

He also refers to Mannerist architects such as Giulio Romano and Vignola and makes a special mention of Michelangelo's highly mannered staircase located in the Laurentian Library in Florence:

The staircase of the Laurenziana is quite overpowering, compressed as it is into so small, high and square a space. All the implications of normality are quite destroyed by this device of putting the stair in a well in such a way that one cannot easily approach it.

Bawa's dissertation focused mainly on Neumann's handling of space and his manipulation of light and, though staircases do not figure prominently in his text, they are generously represented in the accompanying illustrations. These include numerous photographs of the staircases in the palaces of Brühl and Bruchsal, in the Residenz of Würzburg and on the hillside below the Würzburg Käpelle. He was fascinated by Neumann's manipulation of space and his use of light to articulate surfaces. He also celebrates the fusion in Würzburg of Neumann's great staircase with the painted ceiling by the artist Tiepolo to create a *gesamtkunstwerk*.

FROM LEFT TO RIGHT: Meditation path, Ritigala Forest Monastery. Main stair and frescoes, Residenz, Würzburg. The foyer of the Paris Opera House. Bernini's staircase in the Palazzo Barberini, Rome. Michelangelo's stairs in the Laurentian Library, Florence. Donald Friend painting of the city of Galle.

Bawa's interest in the architectural heritage of Sri Lanka can be traced back to early excursions in the family motor car to the ancient cities during the 1930s and to journeys with his brother Bevis during the early 1950s. However, a serious interest developed only after he qualified as an architect in 1957. It was then that he came under the influence of Australian painter Donald Friend who stayed for five years on his brother Bevis's estate at Brief. Friend travelled the length and breadth of the island, recording everything that he saw in sketch books and it was he who encouraged Bawa to look at his native Sri Lanka and its architecture with new eyes. Friend also inspired Bawa's young associate, Danish architect Ulrik Plesner, to undertake a series of measured drawings of medieval buildings that would influence Bawa's thinking and would later contribute to his evolving design philosophy. And, later, he was influenced by archaeologist Senake Bandaranayake whose published dissertation brought previous archaeological records into a unified and comprehensive framework.

It can be said that Bawa's earliest work was heavily influenced by his time at the Architectural Association in London and by his interest, not only in Italian Mannerist and German Baroque architecture, but also in mid-20th-century Modernism. However, following his early experiments in Tropical Modernism, after 1962 he became more and more drawn to the architectural traditions of his native Sri Lanka and began to incorporate indigenous elements into his evolving regionalist style.

Bawa's career spanned from 1958 to 1998 and during that time he designed and built literally hundreds of staircases, from steep and narrow flights in private houses to broad sweeps of stairs in public buildings and gardens. Every one of his staircases was unique and he seldom repeated a design. Whereas a typical new university campus in the West would have employed a restricted number of standard staircase designs, the new University of Ruhunu, built by Bawa during the 1980s, contains an astonishing variety of unique staircases, each one tailored to its particular situation and function.

It is the variety and sheer inventiveness of Bawa's staircase designs that have inspired us to produce this book. We wanted to connect his staircase designs back to the Italian and German staircases that he studied whilst researching his dissertation and to the Sri Lankan staircase tradition that he later came to know and appreciate. We therefore have divided the book into two parts. The first part describes and illustrates some of the staircases in Italy, Germany and Sri Lanka on which Bawa drew for inspiration. The second part describes and showcases staircases, for both public and private projects, that Bawa designed himself between 1958 and 1998.

Towards Architecture

Geoffrey Bawa was born in Sri Lanka in 1919, the second son of a successful Anglo-Moslem lawyer called Benjamin Bawa and his Eurasian wife, Bertha Marion Schrader. Benjamin Bawa died soon after Geoffrey's birth, and Geoffrey and his elder brother Bevis were brought up by their mother in Chapman House, a large colonial mansion on Colombo's then fashionable Darley Road. Geoffrey's cousin, Barbara Anderson, described Chapman House as: "A two storey house with a beautiful staircase that had two landings and lovely banisters to slide down. Geoffrey had a magnificent Hornby trainset which ran from his bedroom out on to the veranda and back along the central corridor".

Geoffrey first pursued a career as a lawyer and came late to architecture. In 1938, at the age of 19, he was sent to England by his mother to study. Having negotiated a place to read English at St Catherine's College, Cambridge for the following autumn, he spent the winter of 1938 in Paris with a distant cousin of his father called Georgette Camille and through her met famous artists such as Braque and Léger. Ignoring the growing threat of war, he then set out on travels through Greece and Italy before returning to Britain to start his university studies.

In Cambridge he led the life of a dilettante. He avoided rugby and rowing and developed an interest in interior design. His remodelling of his Trumpington Street apartment was widely admired, and he was invited by Cambridge friends to their country homes where he discovered the arcane beauty of the English landscaped garden.

In 1942 Geoffrey moved to London to study law in the Inner Temple and, after being called to the Bar in 1944, embarked, without enthusiasm, on a legal career. Returning to Colombo in 1946, he worked briefly in the office of lawyer Noel Gratien. His mother died soon after his return and, after selling much of his property, he quit Sri Lanka and set out on a world tour which took him eastwards to the United States and finally to Europe. In Italy he tried to buy a villa overlooking Lake Garda with the aim of creating his own Italian garden, but he was thwarted by the machinations of Italian lawyers and returned home, in 1948, just as Sri Lanka was casting off the shackles of empire.

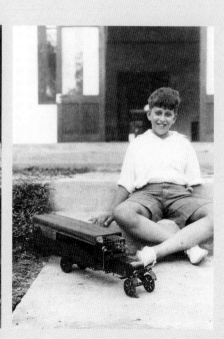

Geoffrey, now homeless, threw himself on the mercy of his elder brother Bevis. Bevis was ten years his senior and had carved out a career as equerry to a succession of British governors. He had been given a rubber estate called Brief by their mother and had created a magical garden around its bungalow. He invited Geoffrey to stay there and suggested that he try to find a similar estate for himself. Geoffrey was impressed by Brief and decided to create a garden of his own, bigger and better than that of his brother. Aided by Bevis, he found an abandoned rubber estate a few miles inland from the coastal town of Bentota, and, having negotiated to buy it from a clan of separate owners, renamed it Lunuganga which translates as 'Salt River'.

The project to transform the eight-hectare estate into a garden would occupy Geoffrey for the next 50 years. The hilly topography suggested the creation of terraces at different levels and necessitated the construction of a number of staircases. As work on the garden progressed, however, he was hampered by his lack of technical knowledge and friends advised him to study architecture. One of his first visitors, early in 1949, was Georgette Camille who urged him: "Become an architect! Then you'll be able to use other people's money to develop your ideas."

Geoffrey's metamorphosis from reluctant lawyer to architect did not occur overnight. There was no Damascene moment. He hesitated for four years before travelling to London in 1953 to enrol as a student at the Architectural Association in London where, having persuaded the Head of School to admit him to the third year of the five-year course, he was a student from 1954 to1957.

The fact that Geoffrey came to architecture from garden design inspired him to work closely with nature. From the outset he was concerned with 'place-making'. He always tried to locate buildings carefully within their setting, to relate them to the surrounding topography and landscape, to set up a dialogue between inside and outside and to develop the spaces between and around buildings as outdoor rooms. His architecture was unashamedly

OPPOSITE, LEFT TO RIGHT: Geoffrey Bawa's parents in a dog cart in front of Chapman House, *circa* 1908. Bawa's parents with his brother Bevis, *circa* 1910. Geoffrey Bawa with a toy Meccano bus, *circa* 1918.

RIGHT, LEFT TO RIGHT: Geoffrey Bawa in his Cambridge rooms, *circa* 1940. Geoffrey Bawa in Italy, *circa* 1956.

picturesque, in the sense that he conceived designs as a series of tableaux that changed according to the point of view.

This approach led him inevitably to conceive of building interiors in a scenographic manner — he imagined them as an *enfilade* of interconnected spaces to be moved through at will, offering a sequence of varying vistas and a variety of volumes of differing proportions modulated by ever changing interactions with light and shade. For him a building was like a filmset and its user was the moving camera.

A logical consequence of this theatrical approach was an interest in staircases. After all, a staircase is potentially the most theatrical element of a building. It exists in four dimensions: the two dimensions of its plan, the third vertical dimension and the fourth dimension of time which marks the progression from one level to another. Such thinking was certainly present in the minds of the great architects of Renaissance Italy and Baroque Germany and also influenced the architects of the Modern Movement. Marcel Duchamp's painting 'Nude Descending a Staircase' of 1912 aptly expresses the Futurists' interest in the dynamic potential of staircases.

What became eventually almost an obsession with staircases was inspired initially by Bawa's early interest in the Mannerist architecture of the Italian Renaissance and in the architecture of the German Baroque. Later, after returning to Sri Lanka at the end of the 1950s, he began to look with renewed interest at the staircases which played such an important role in the architectural and landscape traditions of his native Sri Lanka.

BELOW, CLOCKWISE FROM TOP LEFT: The cascade and pineapple pavilion, Brief, *circa* 1948. The original estate bungalow, Lunuganga, 1948. A student project by Geoffrey Bawa, executed whilst he was at the Architectural Association in London, 1956. During his time at the Architectural Association, Bawa discovered the work of European Modernists such as Le Corbusier: this shows the spiral stair and ramp in the Villa Savoie, 1958. An early view of the entrance steps at Lunuganaga.

OPPOSITE: The north veranda and terrace of the bungalow at Lunuganga.

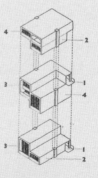

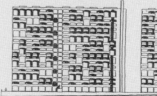
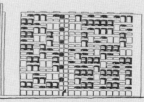

Staircases of the Italian Renaissance

Whilst enrolled at the Architectural Association, Geoffrey spent much of his third and final year of study in Rome, whence he would make occasional trips back to London in his Rolls Royce in order to show his face and see his tutors. He felt very much at home in Italy and learned to speak Italian. Later he would design an Italian villa for his friend the sculptor Lidia Duchini, but the project was sadly nipped in the bud by her untimely death.

During his time in Rome he visited the key buildings of the Italian Renaissance and came to admire the magnificent Mannerist staircases of Bernini, Borromini and Vignola. He also made a point of visiting the great Renaissance gardens that were situated within striking distance of the city, including those of the Villa Lante near Vitterbo and the Villa Farnese at Caprarola, as well as the bizarre 'Garden of Monsters' of the Villa Orsini at Bomarzo.

OPPOSITE: Vignola's Scala Regia in the Villa Farnese, Caprarola.

RIGHT AND FAR RIGHT: Count Orsini's Garden of Monsters, Bomarzo.

THE SPANISH STEPS, ROME

When he lived in Rome, Geoffrey's apartment was situated near to the Spanish Steps, one of the most celebrated outdoor staircases of the Italian Baroque. This monumental composition was created during the 17th century to connect the Piazza di Spagna up to the church of Trinità dei Monti and was completed in 1726.

It comprises a series of flights, each of 12 steps, linking a succession of platforms and moving peristaltically up the hillside. The first three flights, subdivided by balustrades, rise from a fountain in the form of a boat known as the Fontana della Barcaccia. The next broad flight rises to an oval piazza before dividing into two pairs of lateral flights that arrive at a broad transverse platform. Two central flights then connect to a landing from which two stairs of the three flights curve outwards to the topmost platform. Finally, a pair of straight flights rises up to the piazza in front of the church.

Although acting as an important link between two quite separate levels of the city, the Spanish Steps were far more than simply a convenience, offering a meandering ascent from terrace to terrace and affording ever-changing vistas of the city.

OPPOSITE AND RIGHT: Perhaps one of the most famous staircases in the world: the Spanish Steps in Rome, seen (left) before the tourists arrive at sunrise and (right) at midday.

THE CAPITOLINE HILL, ROME

The Capitoline Hill, one of the seven ancient hills of the city, lies to the immediate west of the Forum and was once crowned by an ancient citadel. During the 16th century it was remodelled by Michelangelo Buonarroti who re-oriented it away from the Forum towards the Basilica of St Peter's. Its summit is crowned by three buildings that together define the trapezoidal Piazza del Campidoglio: the Palazzo Senatorio (Senatorial Palace) occupies the centre and is flanked by the Palazzo Nuovo and the Palazzo dei Conservatori. The piazza, designed by Michelangelo, is tiled with an exploding geometric pattern contained within an oval. Michelangelo also designed a new facade for the Palazzo Senatorio with twin flights of steps rising symmetrically to the central entrance on the main upper floor, and designed the Palazzo Nuovo on the piazza's north side.

The piazza is reached by Michelangelo's majestic staircase, the Cordonata, that rises up from the Via del Teatro di Marcello, widening gently to add to the perspective game set up by the trapezoid of the piazza. A *cordonata* is a staircase composed from wide sloping treads and low rises that could be used by horses and donkeys. The Capitoline *cordonata* is flanked to the north by the Aracoeli staircase, a steeper flight that rises up from the street with a total of 124 marble steps to the front of the church of Santa Maria in Aracoeli. It is said that if you climb this staircase on your knees you will enhance your chances of winning the national lottery! The conflicting perspectives of the two staircases offer a visual delight.

Michelangelo's composition probably appealed to Geoffrey because of the way that it proceeded from a formal and symmetrical *parti*, but then broke the symmetries in order to accommodate the constraints of the site.

LEFT: An 18th-century view of the Aracoeli staircase and Michelangelo's Cordonata, attributed to the School of Giovanni Antonio Canal.

OPPOSITE TOP: View of Michelangelo's Cordonata on the right and the Aracoeli staircase on the left.

OPPOSITE BELOW LEFT: The top of the Cordonata with the Piazza del Campidoglio and the Palazzo Senatorio beyond.

OPPOSITE BELOW RIGHT: The final flight of steps on the east flank of the Palazzo Nuovo.

DOUBLE HELIX RAMPS OF THE BELVEDERE PALACE, THE VATICAN

There are a number of famous staircases within the Vatican, including Bernini's Scala Regia which was inserted into the gap between St Peter's Basilica and the Vatican to connect the Basilica with the Sistine Chapel. Perhaps the most remarkable, however, is the double spiral of intertwined ramps built in 1505 by the architect Donato Bramante. This connected the papal apartments of the Vatican's Belvedere Palace down to street level and made it possible for the Pope to access his apartments on horseback or in a palanquin. The double spiral permitted upward and downward travel to proceed independently. The circular ramps, surfaced in herringbone brickwork, were contained within a square tower around a circular well and were supported on Ionic columns.

Geoffrey Bawa would later use a double spiral in his design for the Steel Corporation Tower at the Colombo Industrial Exhibition in 1965.

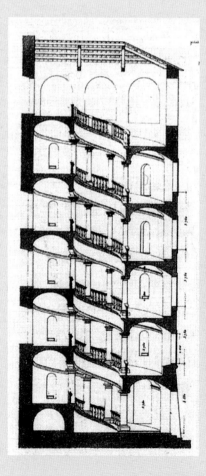

FAR LEFT: A drawing of Bramante's helical ramps in the Vatican's Belvedere Palace. They were designed to enable the Pope to be carried up from street level by palanquin.

LEFT: The inner spiral of Ionic columns.

BELOW: A 53-year-old Geoffrey Bawa is carried in a improvised palanquin on a site visit to the Beruwana Estate, 1967.

OPPOSITE: The ramps are supported on monolithic Doric columns and finished with a herringbone pattern of bricks.

PALAZZO BARBERINI, ROME

Geoffrey was particularly drawn to the Palazzo Barberini in Rome. The Palace was first conceived by Carlo Maderno and was then completed after Maderno's death in 1629 by his nephew Francesco Borromini and Borromini's great rival, Gian Lorenzo Bernini. It is located on a steep hillside that was once the site of a vineyard.

The front of the house is flanked by two projecting wings which create a *cour d'honneur*, while a single wing at the back frames the upper garden terraces. The *piano nobile* is occupied by a large hall that opens to an oval salon which opens to the rear garden. A long *cordonata* begins in a *porte-cochère* under the palazzo and makes a stately climb to the parterre of the upper rear garden.

Geoffrey was attracted by the way in which the *promenade architecturale* linked inside to outside and front to back, but he was particularly struck by the two staircases that were designed by Bernini and Borromini. In what amounted almost to a competition, the two rival architects each designed a staircase at the junctions between the front wings and the hall. The one on the left by Bernini is based on a rectangular plan and is, by virtue of its size, the more important, while the right staircase, by Borromini, is contained within an oval and is the more elegant.

Borromini's church of San Carlo alle Quattro Fontane is just a few steps away from the Palazzo Barberini and is one of the masterpieces of the Italian Baroque. Borromini literally cut corners in order to shoehorn the church and its cloister on to their tiny site. The church is located at a crossroad that features an elaborate sculptured fountain at each corner. A tiny staircase down to the crypt is squeezed in behind one of the fountains. It is a highly sculptural, curving dog leg which seems to have inspired the staircase in Bawa's 33rd Lane house in Colombo.

OPPOSITE LEFT: The front façade of the Palazzo Barberini, Rome.

OPPOSITE RIGHT: The rear façade of the *palazzo* showing the *cordonata* rising from the *porte-cochère* to the garden.

RIGHT TOP: The square Bernini staircase (left) and the oval Borromini staircase (right) in the Palazzo Barberini.

RIGHT BELOW: The stairs down to the crypt in Borromini's chapel of San Carlo alle Quattro Fontane (left) and a detail of the crypt staircase (right).

THE VILLA GIULIA, ROME

Geoffrey particularly admired the work of the 16th-century Mannerist architect Giacomo Barozzi da Vignola, and made a special study of the Villa Giulia in Rome and the Palazzo Farnese at Caprarola.

The Villa Giulia, built on what was then the edge of Rome for Pope Julius III, was designed by Vignola in the mid 16th century and was completed after his death by Bartolomeo Ammanati. Intended as a place of repose for the Pope, it consisted of a series of pavilions that formed between them a succession of enclosed garden courts. The main entrance pavilion has a sober rectangular front onto the street, but a pair of projecting wings behind form a semi-circular loggia that faces into the first garden court. The second pavilion opens onto a subterranean fountain court, known as the Nymphaeum, reached by a pair of quadrant staircases. It is a piece of pure theatre and was intended to serve as pleasure pavilion where the Pope could relax during the heat of the day.

ABOVE AND OPPOSITE: Three views of the subterranean Nymphaeum in Vignola's Villa Giulia, Rome.

THE VILLA FARNESE, CAPRAROLA

The Villa Farnese was built on the foundations of an unfinished fortress that had been designed by Antonio da Sangalla for the first Cardinal Farnese on the steep hillside above the town of Caprarola. Later, in 1550, the second Cardinal Farnese commissioned Vignola to raise a palatial villa on the foundations. Vignola organised the villa on a pentagonal plan around a circular courtyard and connected it to a series of gardens on the hillside beyond. The whole complex was conceived as a *promenade architecturale* that begins in the town's main street and ends in the woods, high above the villa, at an elegant pavilion known as the Casina del Piacere.

A pair of curving stepped ramps rises up from the main street to a gently sloping trapezoidal piazza. The top of the piazza connects directly to a door that opens into the villa's rusticated base in which were housed a *porte-cochère*, along with stables and services. A symmetrical pair of staircases doglegs out from this lower entrance and returns to meet at an upper entrance on the main entry level that connects through to the central circular court. A whole corner of the bastion is given over to the monumental *scala regia* that spirals around a central void, flanked by pairs of Doric columns, and connects the basement and entry levels up to the *piano nobile*. Five smaller spiral staircases are hidden around the central court and connect to all five levels of the villa. On the *piano nobile*, one of the five sides is given over to a loggia that overlooks the town, while the two opposite sides each contain suites of rooms that are connected across moats by bridges to separate garden parterres.

The left-hand parterre runs to the foot of a wooded hillside whence an avenue climbs up through the trees towards the *giardino segreto* or secret garden. Two parallel flights of steps, contained between high flanking walls, run up on either side of a stepped rill or 'water staircase' formed by writhing dolphins to terminate in a semi-circular fountain court. Behind this, a pair of curving stairs climbs up around the fountain to the parterres that front the Casina del Piacere. The *casina* (or summerhouse) is built into the hillside and presents a two-storey front towards the parterres and a single storey front towards an upper garden court at its rear. A final garden court terminates in an exedra set against the hillside.

FAR LEFT: The front façade of Vignola's Villa Farnese in Caprarola, showing the entrance to the basement *porte-cochère* and the twin stairs rising up to the ground-floor entrance.

LEFT: One of the curving *cordonata* that rise up from main street of Caprarola to the piazza in front of the basement *porte-cochère*.

OPPOSITE: Four views of the Scala Regia, the main stair in the Villa Farnese that links the basement level, the entrance level and the *piano nobile*.

OPPOSITE: The twin stairs, flanking the dolphin rill, that connect the wooded walk up to the fountain court and eventually to the parterre fronting the lower level of the Casina del Piacere.

RIGHT: A staircase, flanked by a balustrade formed by another dolphin rill that connects the lower side parterre of the Casina del Piacere up to its upper rear parterre.

GARDENS OF THE VILLA LANTE, NEAR VITERBO

Vignola is also credited with the designs of the Villa Lante at Bagnaia near Viterbo to the north of Rome, built during the 1570s. His client, Cardinal Gambara, had acquired an area of wooded hills to the south of the town and wanted to create a summer residence and hunting lodge.

Vignola proposed creating a relatively small formal garden which stepped up the hillside from the town and served as a prelude to a much larger area of less formal woodland. A pair of compact square pavilions provided accommodation while the garden was conceived as a series of outdoor rooms. Below the villas a large square formal parterre is arranged around a circular pool with a fountain at its centre in the form of a massive bowl, held aloft by statues of four Moors.

Above the villas, the garden steps up on a series of terraces connected by elaborate staircases with fountains, rills and pools. One terrace is arranged as an outdoor dining room with a water channel cut into the top of its long stone table.

The garden impressed both Geoffrey and his brother Bevis and inspired Bevis to incorporate a rill in his garden at Brief. For Geoffrey it opened up the possibilities of creating a stepped landscape of terraces and staircases, with buildings playing a secondary role within a matrix of outdoor rooms.

TOP LEFT: The lower parterre of the Villa Lante with the town of Bagnaia beyond.

TOP RIGHT, BOTTOM LEFT AND BOTTOM RIGHT: Three views of staircases in the mid-level gardens of the Villa Lante.

OPPOSITE: A stepped rill, flanked by staircases, that links two levels of the upper garden. The rills play to all the senses: they add a visual sparkle and the sound of the water, but also serve to cool the air.

GARDENS OF THE VILLA D'ESTE, TIVOLI

The gardens of the Villa d'Este at Tivoli were developed by Cardinal Ippolito d'Este who, after his failed bid to be elected Pope, was made Governor of Tivoli in 1549. This position gave him jurisdiction over the ruins of Hadrian's Villa which he restored with the architect Pirro Ligorio, though he was not averse to removing statuary to his own private collection. As Governor, he was given an official residence in the form of a Benedictine convent that occupied a site on the edge of the town above a steep hillside with panoramic views over the surrounding countryside. Ippolito converted this into his palace. He then instructed Ligorio to remodel the hillside as a complex of hanging gardens arranged on a grid of terraces with grottoes, arcades and staircases, interspersed with pools, water jets and fountains. The water features were fed from a huge cistern at the top of the hillside which was filled via tunnels from a specially constructed aqueduct.

Bawa was impressed by the layout of the garden, but he never attempted to reproduce its water features. This may have been because his own garden, although located in the wettest part of Sri Lanka, straddled a waterless hill and relied on a windmill to pump even a basic domestic water supply.

LEFT: The steep hillside of the Villa d'Este is criss-crossed with ramps and staircases that connect the various levels.

OPPOSITE: Fountains and cascades that form the east end of the villa's main transverse terrace.

OVERLEAF: Three views of a spiral staircase in the Villa d'Este.

Staircases of the German Baroque — Balthasar Neumann

During his year in Rome, Geoffrey elected to write his final dissertation on the work of Balthasar Neumann, the celebrated engineer/architect of the German Baroque.

Johann Balthasar Neumann (1687–1753) was born in Eger (now known as Cheb) in Bohemia and began his career working in a cannon foundry. In 1711 he moved to Würzburg were he joined the local militia and trained as a military engineer. He seems then to have developed a specialisation in architecture and in 1720 was entrusted by Prince Bishop Schönborn with the planning and construction of a new Bishops' Palace in Würzburg. Over the following decades Neumann became the favoured architect of various Prince Bishops in southern Germany and executed a number of designs for palaces and churches.

Geoffrey's research required him to drive in his Rolls Royce across the Alps to Bavaria. He made a special study of Neumann's churches, most particularly that of the Vierzehnheiligen near Bamberg, admiring the quality of light that they achieved. But he also visited the Residenz of the Prince Bishops in Würzburg and the Bishops' Palace at Bruchsal, marvelling at their staircases.

Geoffrey's dissertation was supervised by John Summerson and was submitted in June 1957 under the title "Balthasar Neumann and his Architecture". It describes the construction of the palaces of Würzburg and Bruchsal and contains photographs of the stairs in both palaces.

OPPOSITE: The *porte-cochère* in the Würzburg Residenz showing the foot of the great staircase.

RIGHT: Geoffrey Bawa in his Rolls Royce in Germany, *circa* 1956.

FAR RIGHT: The interior of Balthasar Neumann's church of Fourteen Saints (Vierzehnheiligen).

THE RESIDENZ, WÜRZBURG

The Residenz in Würzburg had been badly damaged during the War and was still undergoing reconstruction when Geoffrey visited it. It was built within the town's fortifications and consisted of two substantial lateral wings connected by a central *corps de logis* to form an imposing *cour d'honneur* facing the town.

The main staircase is one of the most monumental of the German Baroque and takes up almost half of the *corps de logis*, linking the central *porte-cochère* up to the 'White Hall' and the 'Imperial Hall' above. The *porte-cochère* is covered by the low vaults which support the White Hall above and contrasts with the loftiness of the staircase. Its clear column-free area allowed coaches to deposit their passengers and turn around before exiting back to the *cour d'honneur*.

Measuring 18 metres by 30 metres, the stairwell is larger than either of the halls that it serves and is capped by an immense vaulted ceiling that carries frescoes by the Italian artist Giovanni Battista Tiepolo and provides lasting proof of Neumann's engineering skills.

The stair rises in a single central flight to a half-landing before dividing into two separate flanking flights that return to an upper gallery. This surrounds the well of the staircase on all four sides and connects to the White Hall and beyond it the Imperial Hall. The northern end of Tiepolo's vast fresco can be seen from the first half-flight and features Apollo rising into the sky above a circular temple, while the southern end is seen from the return half-flights and focuses on a portrait of the building's patron, Carl Phillip von Greiffenclau. Tiepolo's *trompe l'oeil* effects skilfully bring the heavens down to meet the entablature of the enclosing walls. An image of the architect Neumann in military uniform can be seen, poised astride a cannon between ceiling and wall — a reference to his early career as a cannon founder. He is looking nervously at the vast span of the vault above as if wondering whether his daring structure will hold. In fact, in spite of its huge span, it survived Allied bombing during the Second World War.

This exercise in ostentatious theatricality was intended to impress on visitors the wealth and importance of the Prince Bishop. The stair treads were so deep and shallow that the Bishop could ascend them on horseback or in a palanquin. Far from simply providing the means to move from one level to another, the staircase functioned as a place of congregation and ceremony. Visitors would climb to the half-landing under the gaze of the crowds lining the balcony above and would then turn to be confronted with the magnificent Tiepolo ceiling. This sequence from ground-floor *porte-cochère* to the White Hall above, choreographed under Tiepolo's magnificent ceiling, would later inspire Geoffrey to create the magical entrance to the Bentota Beach Hotel in 1968. It may also have been in his mind some ten years later when he designed the President's staircase in the Sri Lankan Parliament.

BELOW: General exterior view of the Residenz in Würzburg.

OPPOSITE: The upper flights of the grand staircase in the Wurzburg Residenz with Tiepolo's painted ceiling. A portrait of Balthasar Neumann can be seen above the entablature to the right of centre.

THE KÄPPELE, WÜRZBURG

Geoffrey was also impressed by the Pilgrimage Chapels or Käppele that Neumann built to the west of Würzburg on a steep hillside above the River Main. These are reached by an elaborate series of five small piazzas that step up the slope to a final piazza in front of the church. Each piazza is framed by two or three small pilgrimage chapels, each one containing a Station of the Cross. Twin flights of stairs wrap around either side of each central chapel and join together behind it to form a single flight up to the next piazza, creating a peristaltic movement up the hillside.

A mini-version of such an ascent was added to the garden of Bawa's Lighthouse Hotel by his collaborator Channa Daswatte.

LEFT: Two views of the stepped pilgrimage chapels.

OPPOSITE: The pilgrimage church in Würzburg with the topmost of the chapels.

STAIRCASES IN THE PALACE OF BRUCHSAL

The Palace of Bruchsal was commissioned by the Prince Bishop of Speyer at the beginning of the 1720s. It was given a fairly conventional plan with a central *corps de logis* and two projecting wings that formed an entrance court. At a late stage in its construction the Prince Bishop demanded that a connecting mezzanine floor be added between the two reception halls, thus upsetting original plans for a conventional grand staircase at the centre of the *corps de logis*.

Balthasar Neumann was brought in to solve the problem in 1728. He created a pair of curving staircases within an oval drum that borrowed light from two internal courtyards and rose up to a large oval landing that linked the two halls below an oval dome. The result came to be recognised as one of the crowning achievements of the German Baroque.

The great staircase only connected the ground floor to the *piano nobile* of the palace: two other flanking staircases provided the links to all of the subsidiary floors. Although much less ornate than the central staircase, these take the form of short flights with winders and reveal a simple elegance that must have impressed Bawa when he saw them.

BELOW LEFT: One of the secondary staircases in the Palace of Bruchsal.

BELOW RIGHT: A view of one of the curving flights of the main staircase showing its relationship to the central vestibule.

OPPOSITE TOP: The pair of curving flights of the main staircase with the passage through to the central vestibule.

OPPOSITE BELOW: Three views of the curving flights of the main staircase.

Sri Lanka's Architectural Heritage

Sri Lanka is a relatively small island, measuring about 440 kilometres from north to south and 220 kilometres from east to west, but its southern half is dominated by a mountain massif that rises steeply to a height of 2,525 metres, and even its relatively low-lying northern plains are studded with isolated mountain peaks and chains of rocky outcrops.

Early settlements exploited the low-lying land of river valleys for agriculture, but houses were built on higher ground often in and around rocky outcrops. The first Buddhist monasteries were also established on higher ground in caves and under boulders. The rugged landscape produced a need for staircases; thus staircases, often cut directly into the naked rock, became important elements of the architecture and landscapes of the island.

The city of Anuradhapura developed as the prime urban centre during the 5th century BC. It became the focus of a great civilisation that endured for more than a millennium, embracing the northern and eastern parts of the island. Though it finally faltered in the face of invasions from India during the 10th century, there was a brief renaissance during the 11th and 12th centuries when the capital was shifted some 75 kilometres eastwards to Polonnaruwa. This long period of prosperity and growth produced architecture of great sophistication.

The eventual collapse of the Polonnaruwa kingdom in the face of further Indian incursions during the 13th century led the Sinhalese to abandon their traditional homelands and seek refuge in the hills to the south. There followed a period of instability during which the capital was moved several times before eventually being established in Kandy during the 15th century. This period was characterised by a more ephemeral architecture. From the beginning of the 16th century Sri Lanka fell under increasing foreign control first by Portuguese, then Dutch and finally British colonisers.

OPPOSITE: An aerial view of Anuradhapura showing the Ruwanwelisaya stupa in the foreground.

DELVING INTO THE PAST

Geoffrey Bawa's father was a successful lawyer and one of the first motor car owners of Sri Lanka. Following his lead, both of his sons developed a passion for cars, both owned a succession of Rolls Royces, and both enjoyed using them to tour the island. However, Geoffrey's interest in the architectural heritage of Sri Lanka didn't develop until after he bought the Lunuganga garden in 1948 and came to the fore after 1957 when he returned from his studies at the Architectural Association and began to practise as an architect. This interest was encouraged by the Australian artist Donald Friend who stayed with Geoffrey's brother Bevis at Brief for five years from 1957. Donald and Bevis travelled around the island together, searching for what were then little known and remote ruins that Friend recorded in his drawings and paintings.

In early 1959, Geoffrey was joined in his practice by a young Danish architect called Ulrik Plesner. Plesner teamed up with their mutual friend, the textile designer Barbara Sansoni, to record old buildings, enlisting the help of Bawa's assistants, Laki Senanayake and Ismeth Raheem. Together they tracked down and measured forgotten examples of architecture from Sri Lanka's past. Plesner used simple but accurate surveying techniques and developed a way of drawing that was influenced by Donald Friend.

Although Geoffrey took no active part in this project, he gave it his support and took a close interest in its results. Sansoni and Senanayake continued to record buildings for another 20 years, and in the 1980s came together with Sansoni's husband Ronald Lewcock and architect C Anjalendran to produce the book *Architecture of an Island* which was eventually published in 1998.

BELOW LEFT TO RIGHT: Artist Laki Senanayake. Barbara Sansoni displaying one of her drawings. Bevis Bawa (second from left) and Geoffrey Bawa (centre) with one of the family cars. The Nelum Pokuna (stepped lotus pond) in Polonnaruwa. Rock-cut stair in the Vessagiriya Monastery, Anuradhapura.

In 1968 Geoffrey Bawa wrote what would be his only detailed statement about his approach to architecture. It first appeared in the *Times of Ceylon* Annual in an article entitled 'A Way of Building' alongside descriptions of a handful of his projects, and later reappeared as the introduction to the monograph on his work that was published in Singapore by Concept Media in 1986. It included the following observation:

"I have looked into the past for the help that previous answers can give. By this I mean all the past, from Anuradhapura to the latest buildings in Colombo — the whole range of effort, the peaks of beauty and simplicity and the valleys of pretension. When you look at the better examples of what remains of these earlier buildings you will find that they all look life in Ceylon squarely in the face."

Geoffrey later became a friend of the archaeologist Senake Bandaranayake whose seminal book *Sinhalese Monastic Architecture* appeared in 1974. Although his earlier work had focused on religious buildings, Bandaranayke was actively involved in detailed excavations of the pleasure gardens at Sigiriya, and he shared with Bawa his insights into the history of Sri Lankan garden architecture and landscape design and his observations about the relationship between buildings and topography.

MIHINTALE

According to tradition, the Emperor Asoka, ruler of the vast Mauryan Empire, sent his son, Mahinda, to carry the teachings of the Buddha from India to Sri Lanka. In 247 BC Mahinda is said to have accosted the Sinhalese king, Devanampiyatissa, whilst he was hunting in the hills a few kilometres to the east of Anuradhapura and convinced him to adopt the new religion. The people of Sri Lanka soon followed his lead and have remained predominantly Buddhist to this day.

Soon after his conversion Devanampiyatissa founded a monastic community at the place of his conversion which became known as Mihintale or 'Mahinda's Mountain'. Mihintale in fact consists of a cluster of four peaks, all of them accessible by a system of linked staircases. Reaching the highest peak, Mihintalekande, involves a total climb of 200 metres over a number of connected staircases with a total of 1,800 steps.

The ascent begins with a broad and magnificent flight of stairs lined by frangipani or aralia trees. These trees, traditionally associated with cemeteries, are not indigenous to Sri Lanka, and were planted by the archaeologist Panaravitana. They later became a favourite of Geoffrey Bawa and served as his signature.

Half way up the first grand flight, side flights branch off on either side, each climbing to a hilltop stupa. That on the right leads to the ruined Kantaka Cetiya, a circular stupa famous for its four carved *vaahalkadas* or cardinally placed altars. The main flight continues to the ruins of a monastery from where another impressive flight of stairs climbs to the terrace of the Ambasthala Vatadage, the stupa that marks the spot where Devanampiyatissa and Mahinda met. From here there is a choice of four staircases — one climbs steeply on rock-cut steps to the Aradhanagala, a meditation rock from which Mahinda preached his first sermon, while a second makes the steep climb via the brilliant white Mahaseya dagaba to the ruins of the Et Vehera or Stupa of the Elephant on the summit of Mihintalekande.

Mihintale is remarkable for its profusion of staircases and for the way in which its peaks were crowned by glistening white dagabas that could be seen from far and wide.

OPPOSITE LEFT: The rocky peak of the Aradhanagala with the white stupa of the Ambasthala Vatadage.

OPPOSITE RIGHT: A lower flight of steps with the Mahasaya stupa in the background.

RIGHT: The main staircase of Mihintale, lined with frangipani trees.

MOONSTONE STAIRCASES

By the middle of the 1st millennium AD there were more than 20 separate monastic foundations in and around Anuradhapura. Of these, the three largest, the Mahavihare, the Abhayagiriya and the Jetavarana, all conformed to the same general pattern. Each functioned like a small independent satellite town. Outer clusters of cells, some incorporating prayer halls and libraries, were laid out around a central cluster of image houses and the *dagabas*.

The Abhayagiriya monastery grew up around a ridge of boulders and caves in an area to the north west of the Anuradhapura citadel. At its peak it stretched about one and a half kilometres from east to west and covered an area of about 250 hectares, functioning almost like a city within a city and housing over 5,000 monks. Its buildings were designed by specialist monks who were guided by strict precedent and by ancient texts. The monastery had its own workshops with metal foundries, potteries and stonemasons' yards and employed its own craftsmen and artists.

The monks themselves lived and studied in monastic precincts, of which more than 30 have been identified within the Abhayagiriya. Individual buildings were raised above the ground on plinths and these were accessed by short flights of stairs. The design of these staircases was subject to a strict set of iconographic rules.

The foot of the staircase was occupied by a semi-circular stone slab known as a 'moonstone'. Moonstones could be plain, but in more important buildings they were decorated with concentric bands of heraldic animals that represented the ascending levels of the cosmos. Typically, the outer band carries tongues of flame; within this is a procession of animals which represent the cycle of birth and death; then comes a creeper which suggests desire; and finally a line of swans. The centre is occupied by a lotus flower which represents the idea of purity emerging unsullied from an impure world.

The moonstone was flanked by a pair of vertical guard stones, sometimes plain, but usually carrying the image of a snake king, his head framed by a five-headed cobra. The steps themselves were supported by platoons of imps and the curving side walls were carved in the form of *makara* or mythical serpents and propped by the 'snake-king' guard stones.

Thus, a staircase was much more than simply a way of climbing from one level to another: it represented the stages of attainment and was recognised as symbolising the transition between the earth and heaven.

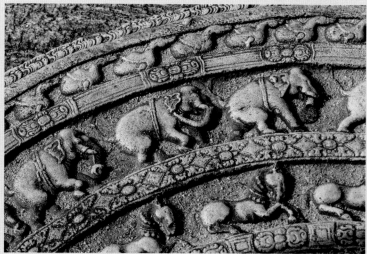

OPPOSITE LEFT: A typical moonstone.

OPPOSITE RIGHT: Detail of a typical moonstone with its concentric rings of swans, elephants and horses.

ABOVE: A typical moonstone staircase in the Abhayagiri Monastery in Anuradhapura.

THE ABHAYAGIRIYA BATHING PONDS

A large monastic complex had to cope with the problems of excess water during the monsoon and water shortage during times of drought. For this reason, the Abhayagiriya is dotted with ponds which functioned both to mitigate against flooding and to act as storage cisterns. In time, these ponds also took on additional functions of ritual, hygiene and recreation.

The Kuttam Pokuna, or Twin Ponds, dating from the end of the 6th century, are located in the north western sector of the monastery. They demonstrate the sophistication of design, construction and workmanship as well as the mastery of hydraulics which characterized the architecture of the later period. The rectangular bathing pools were cut out of the base rock and then lined with immaculately cut tiers of stone which formed continuous steps that descended into the water. Water was fed via a silt trap and through a carved spout into the smaller of the two ponds which was connected via underground conduits to the larger pond. The austere minimalism of the stonework is punctuated only by the carved urns which cap the five pairs of gate posts and a beautifully understated snake-stone which guards the main supply spout.

LEFT: Stairs down to the vast bathing pond in the Abhayagiriya that is known popularly as the Elephant Pond.

OPPOSITE TOP: A view of the more northerly of the Twin Ponds in the Abhayagiriya, Anuradhapura.

OPPOSITE BOTTOM: A staircase on the bund between the Twin Ponds.

THE STAIRCASES OF SIGIRIYA

The citadel palace of Sigiriya is situated half way between the ancient cities of Anuradhapura and Polonnaruwa. It occupies the summit of an outcrop of rock that rears up to a height of some 200 metres above the surrounding boulder-scattered plain. To its east lie the still unexcavated ruins of a walled city, and to its west the ruins of a monumental pleasure garden.

According to legend, the entire complex was built within the space of 17 years during the 5th century by the usurper Kasyapa. Kasyapa had murdered his father, King Datusena, and, fearing retribution, sought to create a stronghold for himself at Sigiriya. After he was killed in battle by his brother, the palace was abandoned and the whole complex was slowly enveloped by jungle.

When it was rediscovered during the 19th century, archaeologists focused their attention on the citadel and on the astonishing wall paintings that graced its western flank. It was only much later that the true extent and nature of the pleasure gardens came to be appreciated.

The royal water gardens cover an area of some 25 hectares and are contained within a double system of moats and ramparts. Laid out on a symmetrical plan which is distorted to accommodate the changing terrain, they constitute one of the most significant examples of Sinhalese garden design. The principal west-east avenue, lined with water channels and fountains, runs from the ramparts to the piles of massive boulders which litter the base of the rock.

These boulders had long been home to hermit monks, but during Kasyapa's time the chaotic tumble of rocks and caves was transformed into a lower annex of the palace: a warren of offices, reception buildings and Buddhist shrines within a maze of narrow alleyways, steep stone staircases, small planted areas, fountain courts and water-courses. From here stone staircases led up to a long gallery which traversed the entire length of the base of the cliff from south to north and connected to a shelf of rock which is now known as the Lion Platform. The gallery is still enclosed by an ancient plastered wall, known as the Mirror Wall, which carries the graffiti comments of countless generations of visitors. Above it, the cliff face was decorated with a series of remarkable wall paintings depicting *apsaras* or heavenly maidens which bear witness to the vibrant school of Sinhalese painting that existed during the 5th century. These can be reached by a vertiginous spiral staircase which dates from the early years of the 20th century.

Access to the summit and the palace was originally via a stone staircase built out from the sheer northern cliff face of the rock. This was contained within a massive brick structure fashioned in the form of a seated lion. Only the massive clawed feet of the lion have survived,

OPPOSITE LEFT: A view of the Sigiriya Rock from the Water Garden.

OPPOSITE RIGHT: A section of the Sigiriya murals showing the 'heavenly maidens'.

RIGHT: A view of the Sigiriya Rock from the north showing the British Period iron staircase rising up from the Lion's Paws.

but these are sufficient to gauge the awesome effect the final ascent must have had on any visitor. The whole composition symbolised Kasyapa's position as king omnipotent of the Sinhalese — the 'lion people'; and master of Sigiriya — the 'lion rock'. Today, the last stage of the climb is made using an ageing metal staircase that hangs precariously from the rock face.

The rock's oval-shaped summit covers an area of about 1.5 hectares and slopes from north to south and from west to east. The palace was conceived as a matrix of linked pavilions with courtyards, gardens and bathing ponds, all aligned to the points of the compass and all falling with the contours on a series of stepped terraces. The remains of stone staircases suggest that several buildings were of two or three storeys.

The summit was divided into three main areas: the palace precinct occupied the highest point at its north-western corner; the public reception buildings were to the north east; and the palace gardens were located towards the south east beyond a large bathing pool. The three areas were connected by a main staircase spine of polished marble that stepped down from the entrance portal in the north to the lower gardens.

The extent to which Geoffrey Bawa was influenced by Sigiriya, and particularly by the planning of the citadel, can be seen in the organisation of the hilltop at Lunuganga and in the layout of the Ruhunu University Campus. All are ordered on an orthogonal grid of terraces that are aligned with the points of the compass and step up and down with the contours, and in each of them the buildings come together to create a series of interconnected 'outdoor rooms'.

OPPOSITE: A view of the Sigiriya Rock from the southwest showing the Mirror Wall that runs below the murals to the Lion Platform.

BELOW LEFT: The feet of the massive lion and the lower section of the stairs that once climbed from the northern platform to the summit.

BELOW RIGHT: The British Period spiral staircase rising up from the Mirror Wall to the murals.

THE POLONNARUWA VATADAGE

The Polonnaruwa Vatadage is situated within a walled precinct known as the Quadrangle that houses a number of striking monuments, including a tooth-relic temple and a large image house known as the Thuparama.

The *vatadage* or roofed stupa evolved as a separate building type during the second half of the first millennium AD. The stupa is typically raised on a series of elevated concentric circular platforms and is surrounded by rings of columns that were clearly intended to support a roof. Although archaeologists have assumed that the roof covered the whole structure, logic and common sense suggest that it covered only the perimeter area used by the worshippers.

The Polonnaruwa Vatadage was rebuilt during the 11th century by King Parakramabahu, which explains its somewhat mannered and highly decorated style. The main outer platform is reached from a porch and staircase that align with the north-south axis of the main tooth relic temple. The raised inner platform is enclosed by a high brick wall and is reached via four cardinally placed moonstone staircases which rise through openings in the wall and meet the four altars that grace the foot of the stupa. There is evidence of four circles of columns, two on the inner platform, one outside of the wall and one on the outer platform.

The Polonnaruwa Vatadage embodies many of the characteristics that we associate with western Baroque architecture — stylised decoration, dynamic movement, dramatic changes of level, imposing staircases, games of light and shade.

LEFT: The Polonnaruwa Vatadage from the air.

OPPOSITE: One of the four cardinal staircase entrances to the main drum of the Polonnaruwa Vatadage showing a moonstone with snake-king guardstones and serpent side balustrades.

YAPAHUWA

During the centuries that followed the collapse of the Polonnaruwa Kingdom, the Sinhalese shifted their capital from place to place and with it the hallowed tooth relic of the Lord Buddha. During the late 13th century, King Bhuvenakabahu I established his capital at Yapahuwa, to the south west of Polonnaruwa. The town nestled at the southern foot of a massive rock and was protected by outer and inner horseshoe-shaped ramparts, giving it the characteristics of a 'mini-Sigiriya'. Little remains of any buildings apart from the ramparts and a stone staircase which rises up from ground level to a broad terrace half way up the rock. Archaeologists are divided about the purpose of the staircase, some arguing that the King's Palace was located at the upper level, others that it housed the Temple of the Tooth.

The staircase is unique because of its excellent state of preservation and because of its stylistic ambiguities. It rises in three steep sections separated by landings. The first section rises in two short flights to a substantial stone platform. The second consists of a long and very steep unbroken straight flight lined by stone plinths. Although the sides of the stair are parallel, the side plinths diminish in width to create a false sense of perspective. The third rises in two separate flights to a pavilion which served as the gatehouse to the main terrace.

The two flights of the uppermost section are flanked by massive stepped walls. The lower flight rises between two solid piers in the form of monastic towers. The halfway landing is guarded by a pair of lions, carved in a style which suggests Cambodian influence. Above them is a pair of *ghajasimha*, mythical hybrids of lions and elephants. The stone gatehouse has been substantially restored and incorporates exquisitely carved columns, engaged and free standing, as well as stone relief panels above the windows. Stone friezes on the flanking walls and on the base of the gatehouse are carved with images of dancers and musicians.

The staircase is remarkable for its steepness. The lower of the two upper flights rises six metres over a length of five metres with 25-cm rises and 21-cm goings. Whilst it might be argued that the steepness was necessitated by the slope of the hillside, it would have been a simple matter to incorporate transverse flights to reduce the angle. The intention, clearly, was to belittle visitors and impress upon them the importance of the king. No doubt the king himself was carried up in a palanquin or used an alternative back route of his own.

OPPOSITE LEFT: The top flight and portal of the staircase at Yapahuwa.

OPPOSITE RIGHT: One of the *ghajasimha* on the top flight of the Yapahuwa staircase.

RIGHT: An aerial view of the staircase at Yapahuwa, showing the three flights and the ruins of the former palace.

MULKIRIGALA

Some 80 kilometres away to the south of Sri Pada and a few kilometres inland from the port of Tangalla, lies the rock of Mulkirigala, the site of an ancient monastery, famous for its temple murals. Like Sri Pada (see pages 70–73) it is a place of pilgrimage. A succession of staircases leads via its various temple caves to the *dagaba* on its summit. However, it is much smaller than Sri Pada, a mere 200 metres above sea level, and there are only 530 steps between its bottom and top.

During the Dutch period, according to legend, travellers seeking to visit Sri Pada would be taken instead by unscrupulous guides to Mulkirigala on a circuitous route from Tangalla. This ruse, it was argued, saved the travellers a great deal of effort and spared them from encounters with wild animals, Kandyan outlaws and the dreaded leeches of the Peak Wilderness.

BELOW AND OPPOSITE: A few of the stair flights of different dates that link the various cave terraces.

MALIGATHENNE

The boulder-strewn mountain of Maligathenne rises dramatically out of a bucolic landscape of paddy fields and low hills and is home to an ancient forest monastery. Yet it lies only a few minutes away from the busy A1 highway and a mere 20 kilometres as the crow flies from the heart of Colombo. Most of its surviving buildings are of fairly recent origin, but the caves behind them have been in continuous use for at least two millennia. Its name means 'palace terrace' and legend has it that it once served as a royal refuge.

A rock-cut staircase climbs up from the village at the foot of the mountain to a series of terraces where the main complex of cave temples is located. Ahead is the biggest cave containing a large seated Buddha. To its left, nestling within a chaotic pile of boulders, are caves which still house hermit monks.

The path to the summit follows an anti-clockwise spiral that is dictated in part by the topography, though the hand of sophisticated landscape artists is clearly evident. Having threaded its way between groups of small hermitages, it dips under a natural arch of rock before ascending through a chasm formed by sheer walls of granite. A final curving rock-cut staircase leads to the summit plateau where a simple white *dagaba* sits beside a stone-cut lotus pond. The summit affords a clear view of Adam's Peak away to the south east, while to the west the towers of Colombo Colpetty are clearly visible and aeroplanes can be seen as they approach Katunayake Airport.

OPPOSITE LEFT: A staircase passing under a natural arch of rock, Maligathenne.

OPPOSITE RIGHT: A staircase passing through a natural chasm.

RIGHT: The final flight of rock-cut steps leading to the summit stupa.

SAMANALA KANDA, SRI PADA, SHIVA PADAM OR ADAM'S PEAK

Probably the most famous and certainly the longest staircase in Sri Lanka is that which climbs to the summit of Samanala Kanda, a conical mountain that lies at the southern edge of the central massif and rises to a height of 2,243 metres. This name refers to its association with the local deity Saman, but also has the meaning 'Butterfly Mountain'. A boulder on its summit carries an indentation that is believed by Buddhists to be the footprint of the Lord Buddha and they refer to the mountain as Sri Pada or "Sacred Footprint". Hindus claim the footprint to be that of Lord Siva, and know the mountain as Shiva Padam. Moslems and Christians attribute it to Adam which accounts for its European name: Adam's Peak.

The mountain has been a place of pilgrimage for more than 1,000 years, and there are several paths that lead to its summit. In recent years, as the number of pilgrims has increased, the main sections have been laid with stone steps while handrails have been added to the steeper flights. The most popular route is from Hatton via Maskeliya to Nallathanniya, where the climb begins in earnest. It is estimated that there are about 5,500 steps between Nallathanniya and the summit. As it nears the top the staircase divides with separate flights leading up and down. Most pilgrims climb by night to avoid the heat of the day and in the pilgrimage season, which runs from December to March, the stairs are lit during the hours of darkness. Climbing at night also holds out the possibility of reaching the summit before dawn and seeing the impressive sunrise which casts a triangular shadow across the surrounding hills.

OPPOSITE: Part of the staircase on the flank of Samanala Kanda.

RIGHT: The summit of Samanala Kanda.

RIGHT: A distant aerial view of
Samanala Kanda.

BAWA'S
BUILT
PROJECTS

BAWA'S STAIRCASES IN SRI LANKA

Almost all of the staircases featured in this chapter were designed and built in Sri Lanka by Geoffrey Bawa and his collaborators between 1958 and 1998.

In 1957, having qualified as an architect at the Architectural Association in London, Bawa returned to Sri Lanka where he was offered a partnership by Jimmy Nilgiriya in the firm of Edwards, Reid and Begg (E, R & B).

Between 1958 and 1967, he operated as a partner of Jimmy Nilgiriya and Valentine Gunasekara, though all three employed their own staff and ran their own projects under the aegis of E, R & B. During this period, he worked closely with the Danish architect Ulrik Plesner who functioned as his de facto associate. The practice had occupied an office in the Prince Building in the Colombo Fort, but in 1963 Bawa moved it to purpose-built premises in Alfred House Road in Colombo's Colpetty. In 1968 he was joined by engineer K Poologasundram who replaced Nilgiria and Gunasekara and remained Bawa's sole partner in E, R & B until 1988.

In 1989 Bawa closed E, R & B and opened a small studio office in his Colombo home on 33rd Lane, where he practised as Geoffrey Bawa and Associates with Channa Daswatte as his principal assistant and later associate. In 1998 he suffered the stroke which ended his career. In the same year the Alfred House offices were converted into what is known today as the Gallery Café.

During the early period, Bawa was assisted by Laki Senanayake, Turner Wickremasinghe, Stanley Perera and Nihal Amerasinghe. After 1965 these were joined by Ismeth Raheem, Pheroze Choksy, Anura Ratnavibhushana, Vasantha Jacobsen and Mahaname Prematilleke. Later assistants included C Anjalendran, Nihal Bodinayake, Dilshan Ferdinando, Sumangala Jayatilleke and Amila de Mel. In addition, Bawa developed close friendships and collaborations with Batik artist Ena de Silva and textile designer Barbara Sansoni.

All of these people contributed immeasurably to the work of the practice, though Bawa remained its central figure and guiding light, functioning as the conductor of an orchestra of many talents.

PREVIOUS PAGE: The main stair in the Triton Hotel (now called the Heritance Ahungalla) with mural by Laki Senanayake.

LEFT: Laki Senanayake's "Battle Staircase" in the Lighthouse Hotel, Galle.

Lunuganga
BENTOTA, 1948–1998

Soon after his return from his world tour in 1948, Geoffrey Bawa bought an abandoned rubber estate a couple of miles inland from Bentota and renamed it Lunuganga or Salt River. His aim was to create a tropical version of an Italian Renaissance garden. Its eight hectares straddled two low hills on a peninsula that jutted out into a brackish lagoon known as the Dedduwa Lake. A dilapidated bungalow sat on the summit of the northern hill surrounded by rubber trees.

The garden project was more of a journey than a destination and Geoffery devoted much of his free time and capital to its development over the next 50 years. However, his plans changed from year to year in response to new ideas and new discoveries.

Early photographs show that his first ideas were rooted in Europe: the staircase up to the southern terrace, for instance, was originally Baroque in spirit and only later took on its more modern and abstract fan form. As the garden developed, Geoffrey became more and more influenced by his native Sri Lanka, both by its natural beauty and by its great landscape traditions. Lunuganga became, in his words, "a garden within the greater garden of Ceylon". Not a flower garden or a garden of gaudy colours, it is a monochrome composition of green on green, a place of hidden surprises, of sudden views and of panoramic vistas.

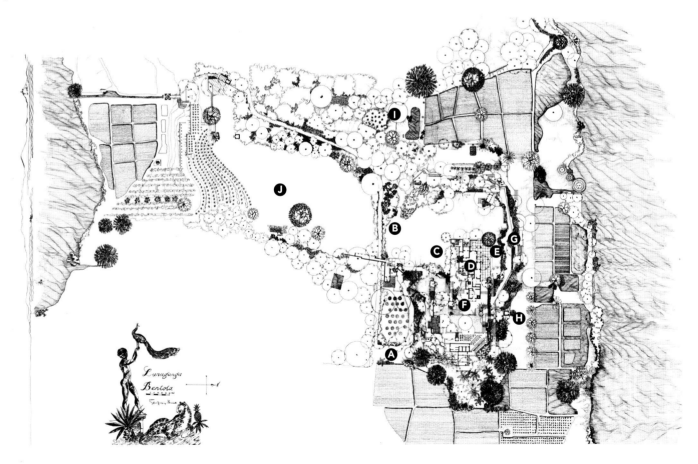

A	The Entrance	F	The Eastern Terrace
B	The Ha-Ha	G	The Cliff
C	The South Terrace	H	The Broad Walk
D	The House	I	The Field of Jars
E	The North Lawn	J	The Cinnamon Hill

From the outset Geoffrey knew that clearing away a swathe of trees from north to south would open up new vistas across the lake in both directions and establish a clear axis across the garden. Achieving this involved not only removing trees but also lowering the summit of the southern hill by about two metres. And to add drama he cut away the north side of the northern hill to create an artificial cliff that fell to a flat area of water meadows and rice paddy.

The summit of the northern hill was then formed into a series of stepped terraces, aligned orthogonally but asymmetrically to match and amplify the contours. In this Geoffrey was following the example of the builders of the Anuradhapura Period and was echoing the arrangement of terraces and staircases that cover the summit of the Sigiriya rock. The original bungalow, cocooned in a girdle of verandas and courtyards, became the centre of a constellation of pavilions, creating a checkerboard of outside spaces.

All of this required a network of pathways and staircases — and there are around 30 separate flights of steps scattered around the garden. A wide meandering staircase rises up through the trees from the car park to the terrace below the glass pavilion; a fan staircase connects that terrace up to the south entrance terrace; staircases tumble down from the Eastern Terrace towards the Broad Walk and the water

OPPOSITE: A plan of the entire estate of Lunuganga.

TOP: A west-east section through the Northern Hill at Lunuganga, looking north, showing how the buildings are married with the topography.

RIGHT: An aerial view of Lunuganga from the north, showing the rice paddy, the cliff and the bungalow.

gardens; cascades of steps, known as the Scala Danesi, weave their way up and down the cliff. In the Sandela, a garden pavilion perched on the southern edge of the Eastern Terrace, a narrow staircase connects up to a balcony with no other purpose than to enhance the scale of the space. And, in Geoffrey's own private bathing courtyard, an equally narrow staircase climbs up to a lookout turret to give a secret view of the garden.

Geoffrey worked on the garden for 50 years until he was felled by a massive stroke in 1998, but he continued to plan changes right up to the end. Today, 20 years later, the garden is maintained by the Geoffrey Bawa Trust and is still very much as Geoffrey left it. Lunuganga is open to the public and functions as a country hotel.

ABOVE AND OPPOSITE: **Two views of the stairs up from the arrival court to the South Terrace.**

OPPOSITE TOP: The South Terrace and the door to the house.

OPPOSITE BOTTOM: Geoffrey Bawa's private bathroom court with the narrow stairs leading up to his secret look-out tower.

RIGHT: Garden steps beneath the frangipani tree on the North Terrace.

ABOVE: Steps leading up to the Kitchen Terrace.

OPPOSITE, CLOCKWISE FROM TOP LEFT: The narrow staircase that climbs steeply up to the mezzanine in the Sandela Pavilion on the Eastern Terrace. A staircase below the Northern Terrace. The staircase in the Gallery (former cowshed). The entrance to the Drafts-men's Pavilion next to the Ha-Ha.

LEFT: One of the paths that cuts across the face of the Cliff.

OPPOSITE TOP: The Roman Pavilion on the western slope of the hill.

OPPOSITE BOTTOM LEFT: The walk at the foot of the western slope leading to the Field of Jars.

OPPOSITE BOTTOM RIGHT: The foot of the Scala Danesi at the base of the Cliff.

The Deraniyagala House
GUILFORD CRESCENT, COLOMBO, 1952–58

Bawa's first commission to design a house came in 1952 while he was still working as a barrister. His clients, the Deraniyagalas, came from ancient aristocratic stock but were also members of a new intellectual elite. They asked Geoffrey to design a house that would reflect their position in society — one foot in the past and one foot in the future.

However, he soon realised that he lacked the necessary technical knowledge and, having decided to go to London to study architecture, advised Mrs Deraniyagala to find another architect. But she had taken a liking to this strange half-lawyer/half-architect and told him that she would wait until he had qualified for him to design her house.

When Geoffrey returned to Sri Lanka in 1957 his first act was to complete the Deraniyagala House. The design was in many ways quite conventional, though it broke the house into interconnected pavilions and incorporated such traditional elements as a long veranda and a small enclosed courtyard.

The staircase in the main pavilion took the form of a free-standing concrete spiral at the end of a long hallway. Such staircases had become the *sine qua non* of modern architecture in Sri Lanka. However, Geoffrey later came to repudiate them, regarding them more as sculptural objects rather than as spatial entities. He never again designed a free-standing spiral for a private house and when he did use a spiral, as in the Ena de Silva House, he enclosed it within a shaft in the manner of Borromini.

LEFT AND OPPOSITE: **The spiral staircase seen from above and from below.**

St Thomas's Prep School
GALLE ROAD, COLOMBO, 1957–62

When Geoffrey first joined Edwards, Reid and Begg in 1957 he was assigned a project to build two classroom blocks for a prep school on the sea side of Galle Road in Colombo-Colpetty.

First to be completed was a three-story block that ran parallel with the railway track and was clad in a breathing wall of hollow blocks. It contained a rather grand staircase with a central half-flight and twin return flights. The landing walls were decorated with murals by Ena de Silva's son, Anil Jayasuriya.

The second block was placed at right angles to the first and relied on deep overhanging eaves and a perimeter balcony to provide shade and rain protection for the classrooms. The balconies supported a continuous concrete parapet that was decorated with concrete reliefs of plants and animals designed by Anil Jayasuriya. The main staircase was a simple straight flight and rose beside a mural by Anil.

TOP LEFT: A view of the two classroom blocks as they appeared in 1960. The relief panels by Anil Jayasuriya on the nearer block no longer exist.

BOTTOM LEFT: The first-floor landing of the main stair in the three-storey block as it was in 1960. The mural by Anil Jayasuriya no longer exists and the open balustrades have been replaced by solid walls.

LEFT: The top landing of the stair in the three-storey block showing the open top floor that once served as a gym.

OPPOSITE: The upper flights of the stair in the three-storey block showing the solid balustrades.

Tennis Club
RATNAPURA, 1959

The Ratnapura Tennis Club occupies a steep site in the woods above the town's Rest House. Bawa designed the Club House to sit above the tennis courts and organised its various constituent parts — bar, changing rooms, tribune — in stepped fashion to exploit the slope. These were then covered by a single roof plane that echoed the fall of the land. Thus the whole building resembled a giant staircase.

The Club House was built on a shoestring: a local builder was employed and used handmade bricks, rubble and jungle timber. And yet, hidden in the woods and almost forgotten, it has survived for 60 years. The tennis courts have been abandoned, but the building is still used as a sports hall and club.

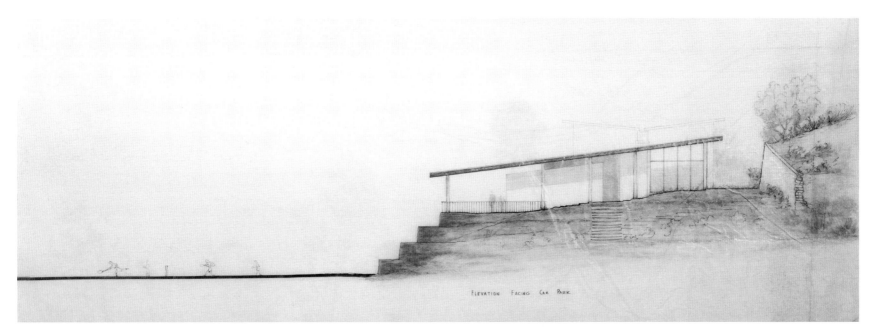

ELEVATION FACING CAR PARK.

OPPOSITE CLOCKWISE FROM TOP: A section drawn through the Tennis Club reveals how the building exploited the slope to act as a tribune. The Club House seen across the tennis courts. View from the Club Room towards the tennis courts. The Club Room in use as a judo gym in 2001.

RIGHT: A view of the stairs leading down from the Club Room to the tennis courts, illustrating the palette of low cost building materials: jungle timber columns, local bricks, cement floors.

The A S H de Silva House

WOODWARD MAWATHA, GALLE, 1959

The A S H de Silva House was built on the outskirts of Galle. The client was a doctor and the house included a surgery. Like the Ratnapura Tennis Club, it was built on a steep slope and was covered by a single roof plane. The house was divided, pinwheel fashion, into four separate pavilions: the main house, an annexe for the doctor's sister, the service quarters, and the doctor's consulting room. Three staircases connect the various levels: one external stair provides a separate access to the sister's annexe; another, running alongside a small internal pool court, connects the two principal levels of the house; a third runs down the hill in a mysterious tunnel to link the house with the surgery.

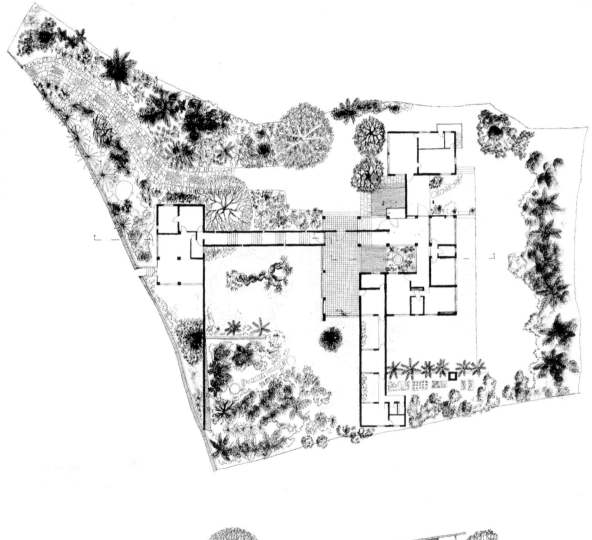

LEFT: The plan adopts a pinwheel form. The main house is arranged as a rectangle around a central pool court. It steps down the steep hillside from right to left and terminates in the doctor's surgery.

OPPOSITE TOP LEFT: The external stair that provides a separate entrance to the sister's annexe.

OPPOSITE TOP RIGHT: A view of the main front door with the sister's stair on left.

OPPOSITE MIDDLE LEFT: The lower pool court.

OPPOSITE MIDDLE RIGHT: An inside view of the staircase link.

The Ena de Silva House
BUILT IN ALFRED PLACE, COLOMBO IN 1961. DEMOLISHED IN 2012.
REBUILT IN LUNUGANGA, BENTOTA IN 2015.

The Ena de Silva House was the first of Bawa's designs to achieve that fusion of traditional and modern that would become his hallmark. Its various pavilions formed between them a series of courtyards which were suggestive of a traditional Sinhalese manor house. However, the openness of the plan was totally modern in its conception. Although the site was to all intents and purposes flat, Geoffrey created a raised threshold in the tunnel between the outer entrance porch and the main courtyard to give an added sense of drama: visitors were led up in order for them to enter with a downward movement.

Two bedrooms are located at first-floor level in the rear pavilion and are reached by means of a spiral staircase. In contrast to the Deraniyagala House, the spiral is contained by flanking walls and the treads are supported on a central timber column. With typical wit, Geoffery exaggerated the sense of enclosure by exploiting the void between two wardrobes to insert a tapering window, thus creating the illusion of a massive wall, recalling Balthasar Neumann's side staircases at Bruchsal. Another narrow staircase with giant treads playfully links the studio up to a mezzanine level.

The house was demolished in 2012, but was carefully rebuilt at Lunuganga by the Geoffrey Bawa Trust in 2016.

LEFT: A view from a bedroom down into the courtyard (*circa* 1961).

OPPOSITE: Three views of the main staircase in its reconstructed state. The spiral is contained within a square well. The deep reveals of the window are formed by the backs of wardrobes and create the illusion of a thick wall.

OVERLEAF FROM LEFT TO RIGHT: Although the site was more or less flat, Bawa played with the levels to create a heightened sense of drama. Here the studio flat is raised two steps above the arcade of the courtyard to gain extra privacy. Two minimalist staircases serving mezzanines in the roof of the front wing.

The Raffel House
WARD PLACE, COLOMBO, 1963

This house was designed for a doctor and his musician wife. The site is land-locked and is entered at one corner from a long narrow lane. The house itself occupies two floors on an 'L' shaped plan and is placed on the site in such a way as to form an entrance court next to the lane and a garden court within the 'L'. The entrance court is entered through an arched barbican connected to the main door by a terracotta pavement under a tiled roof.

A narrow staircase climbs to a secret room above the archway that serves as a study and lookout. The idea of a secret staircase to an upper cell or lookout recurs throughout Geoffrey's work. He built such a staircase in his bathroom court at Lunuganga and provided similar lookouts in his design for the guest pavilions of the Bali Hyatt Hotel.

The main staircase is located strategically at the knuckle of the plan and is in the form of a dogleg with winders that are contained within a square well. It rises up beyond the first floor and breaks through the roof to become a tower with a belvedere. The half-landing performs an elegant curve. The curving hardwood handrail is echoed by steel bands supported on steel posts. The first-floor landing merges with a generous corridor that serves as a reception space. The floors and the stair treads are clad in the same square terracotta tiles.

LEFT: A lightwell in the entrance court where a narrow stair gives access to a secret room above the entrance arch.

OPPOSITE TOP: A view down into the spiral dogleg stair that links the ground floor up to the top floor of the water tower.

OPPOSITE BOTTOM LEFT TO RIGHT: The narrow stair up to the secret room, its balusters of coconut wood. The grand arrival of the main stair on the ground floor. The top flight of the main stair.

St Bridget's Montessori School
MAITLAND CRESCENT, COLOMBO, 1963

St Bridget's Montessori School was one of a number of projects designed for the nuns of Good Shepherd Convent under the guidance of an Irish nun known as Mother Good Counsel. The site was restricted and the brief necessitated building on two storeys. Working with Laki Senanayake, Geoffrey tried to create the feel of a traditional village school with mud walls and overhanging eaves. The concrete perimeter parapet of the first floor is curved in section and perforated with rounded openings to suggest clay construction, while the toilets are contained within concrete igloos. The two staircases are in the form of elongated spirals contained within curving walls, perforated with oval openings at a child's eye-level.

Igloos and stairs were originally of raw concrete decorated with murals by Barbara Sansoni. In time they have been painted with heavy gloss paint and new murals have been added.

Lovingly created by Mother Good Counsel and her architect, the building served successive generations of children for more than 50 years until, tragically, half of it was demolished in 2016 to make way for an unspeakably ugly replacement.

BELOW FROM LEFT TO RIGHT: A view of the first-floor classrooms showing one of the staircases and, beyond it, a toilet pod. The painted walls of the staircases were originally of raw concrete, decorated with reliefs of flora and fauna by Barbara Sansoni.

OPPOSITE: These staircases were constructed of in situ concrete and were made to simulate traditional mud construction, with windows for small children to peer through.

The Polontalawa Estate Bungalow
LANDAWATTE, 1964

This bungalow was built to serve a remote coconut estate near Chilaw that belonged to a Swiss trading company. Director Thilo Hoffmann had initially requested that a simple rectangular bungalow be built on a flat site next to the meeting of two roads. During a site visit, however, Geoffrey persuaded him to shift the project to a nearby cluster of huge boulders. Using sticks and string he then laid out the bungalow as a series of pavilions inserted amongst the boulders. The project architect was Ulrik Plesner.

The main open-sided sitting room occupies the space between two boulders and its roof is supported on a massive concrete beam that spans them. Visitors enter via a lych-gate in the outer wall. From there a route skirts round one rock and dives between two others before slipping under the roof. In a typical parti, Geoffrey choreographed the entrance: visitors were made to climb up from the gateway on a series of steps cut into the rock and then make a grand entrance down a curving staircase between the boulders.

A visitors' bedroom is built against one of the boulders and is reached by a stone staircase, its treads surfaced with terracotta tiles and its handrail and balusters made, appropriately, from coconut timber.

The relationship of the house to its boulder setting is reminiscent of ancient rock monasteries such as that of Vessagiriya in Anuradhapura.

OPPOSITE LEFT: The pathway leading from the entrance gate into the house.

OPPOSITE RIGHT: The house grows out of the site and the roof over the main sitting room spans a pair of massive boulders.

RIGHT: Steps leading down from the entrance path between the massive boulders into the main sitting room.

Geoffrey Bawa's Town House
33RD LANE, BAGATELLE ROAD, COLOMBO

During the 1960s Geoffrey bought a row of four tiny cottages at the end of a lane in the heart of Colombo-Colpetty and proceeded to knock them together to form a single, labyrinthine courtyard house.

The first cottage was demolished to make way for a modernist tower that rose like a periscope above the surrounding roof tops. It contained a carport on the ground floor, a sitting room and guest suite on the first floor, a covered garden terrace on the second floor and an open terrace on the third floor. The three main floors are linked by a highly sculptural dog-leg stair which winds its way from floor to floor. Its surfaces are painted ethereal white and are reminiscent of the curving staircases of Francesco Borromini and Balthasar Neumann. The tower offers an oblique tribute to le Corbusier's Maison Citrohan, and the final stair to the roof is a straight flight contained within a concrete parapet and cantilevered out from the side wall.

LEFT: The moonstone before the front door.

BELOW: The section shows how the converted bungalow contrasts with the new tower over the carport and reveals how Bawa manipulated the levels of the long corridor to add an enhanced sense of theatricality.

OPPOSITE: The staircase in the new tower, perhaps inspired by Borromini's staircase in the crypt of San Carlo in Rome.

OVERLEAF LEFT AND RIGHT: The foot of the main staircase seen from the carport. The landing of the main staircase with the panelled door by Ismeth Raheem

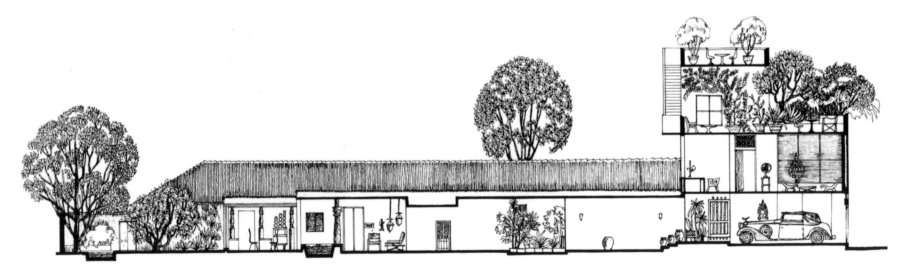

Steel Corporation Tower
INDUSTRIAL EXHIBITION, BULLER'S ROAD, COLOMBO, 1964

In 1965 an Industrial Exhibition was staged on what had been the Colombo Racecourse. Young architects associated with Edwards, Reid and Begg were responsible for designing a number of the local pavilions: Valentine Gunasekara designed a pavilion for Samuel and Sons, Anura Ratnavibhushana and Ismeth Raheem designed the Paper Corporation pavilion, Pheroze Choksy the Tyre Corporation Pavilion, and Geoffrey Bawa the Steel Corporation Pavilion. The two most exciting structures of the exhibition were the circular folded plate planetarium, designed by P W D architect S Kandavel, and the viewing platform designed for the Steel Corporation by Geoffrey Bawa with Anura Ratnavibhushana.

The viewing platform was very loosely inspired by Vladimir Tatlin's unbuilt Russian Constructivist Tower of 1920. It rose to a height of about 40 metres and used steel off-cuts to support viewing platforms on three levels. At its core was a pair of intertwined helical staircases built, unsurprisingly, of steel and inspired directly by Geoffrey's favourite Bramante stair in the Vatican.

Sadly, the tower was later dismantled and few images of it have survived. It must surely have been seen by a young Cecil Balmond, the Sri Lankan born engineer who went on to design the Orbit tower at the 2012 London Olympics.

LEFT: This astonishing tower was designed for the 1965 Industrial Exhibition and was inspired, no doubt, by the unbuilt tower of the Russian Constructivist Tatlin and Bramante's double helix staircase in the Vatican.

Steel Corporation Offices

ORUWELA, 1966

In 1966 the Steel Corporation built a steel rolling mill on a rubber estate to the east of Colombo. Its purpose was to convert imported steel billet into structural sections and a reservoir was created to store the water needed for cooling.

Geoffrey designed an office block that jutted out into the reservoir as well as a canteen with staff changing rooms and an area of staff housing. The main floor of the office building is at the level of the bank of the reservoir, and its lower floor is at water level. This is an early example of the outward stepped section that Geoffrey employed on a number of projects at this time: an upper floor projects out to protect the main floor from sun and rain and is itself protected by deep overhanging eaves. The walls are formed by a grid of openings, some glazed and some open. The entrance led directly to an imposing staircase that steps up on three sides of a central square well.

The building is now empty and is threatened with demolition.

BELOW LEFT: The office building seen across the reservoir.

BELOW MIDDLE: The top landing of the main stair in the office building.

BELOW RIGHT: The lower flight of the main stair in the office building.

Tourist Village and Railway Station
BENTOTA, 1968

In 1997 the Ceylon Tourist Board commissioned Geoffrey Bawa to draw up a master plan for a new beach resort at Bentota, some 60 kilometres south of Colombo. This was in part a response to a new upsurge in tourism that had accompanied the inception of long-haul flights from Europe to Sri Lanka. The site occupied a tongue of land that separated the estuary of the Bentota River from the Indian Ocean and was crossed by the main railway line that linked Colombo to Galle. The master plan identified five hotels of which two, the Bentota Beach and the Serendib, Geoffrey would later design. It also proposed the creation of a tourist village for which Geoffrey went on to design shops, a bank, a police station and a railway station with an elegant concrete bridge that connected the station directly with the beach.

BELOW: A view of the Tourist Village showing the relationship between the shopping street and the raised garden.

OPPOSITE CLOCKWISE FROM TOP: The bridge linking the railway station to the beach. The station platform (the steps were put in later to accommodate new higher rolling stock). Two views of the steps of the railway bridge.

The Beach Hotel

BENTOTA, 1968

The Beach Hotel was one of Geoffrey's most original designs, combining the ambience of a medieval manor house with the functions of a modern tourist hotel. It sat on top of a mound that had once supported a small wooden Dutch fort and, more recently, a rest house. Geoffrey enclosed the hill in a mock stone bastion and placed the main reception spaces around a tranquil pool court on its summit. On top of these he added two upper floors in an 'L' formation so that the individual rooms had views out either to the sea or the estuary. This was at a time when imports were restricted and the plan was ordered in such a way that a single lift could serve every level. Geoffrey, along with his colleagues and friends, designed all the furniture and interior furnishings and supplied the art works. Even the doors of the single lift were handmade by a local craftsman to a design by Anura Ratnvibhushana.

The main entrance sequence was, consciously or unconsciously, inspired by the great staircase in the Würzburg Residenz. Visitors were deposited in a dark vaulted *porte-cochère* from whence they ascended a noble staircase to a reception hall that was roofed with magnificent batik ceiling panels, each one individually made by Ena de Silva to designs by her son Anil Jayasuriya.

A staircase linking the restaurant down to a bar within the bastion was topped by a giant peacock sculpture by Laki Senanayake. The secondary staircases in the wings were designed as elegant dog-legs with winders, and the terrace atop the stone bastion was connected to the garden level by a single flight of stone.

Sadly, the hotel was subjected to a makeover during the 1990s and is now scheduled to be demolished.

LEFT TOP: East-West section through the Bentota Beach Hotel, showing the raised central courtyard and the stepped-out section of the bedroom floors (drawn by Ismeth Raheem, 1969).

BOTTOM LEFT: An aerial photo showing the west wing of the hotel and the swimming pool.

BOTTOM RIGHT: The staircase linking the dining room to the lower bar, presided over by a bronze peacock by Laki Senanayake.

OPPOSITE: The main stair from the *porte-cochère* up to the reception area with Ena de Silva's batik ceiling.

OVERLEAF LEFT TOP: The lower section of the Peacock Stair with its strange disappearing flight.

OVERLEAF LEFT BOTTOM: Views of the secondary staircases in the bedroom wings.

OVERLEAF RIGHT: A view of the hotel from the northwest.

The Serendib Hotel
(aka Awani)
BENTOTA, 1969–71

The Serendib Hotel was intended to serve as the budget cousin of the Beach Hotel and was conceived as a simple rest-house. Its two-storey pavilion faced the sea through a graceful grove of coconut trees and was protected from the railway by a line of service buildings that enclosed a pleasant pool court guarded by peacocks. The upper rooms opened onto generous balconies and were connected to the coconut grove by narrow staircases.

A three-storey wing and swimming pool were later added to the south of the main block alongside an elegant poolside dining pavilion. A curved staircase in the new wing connects to a first-floor corridor that serves the upper two levels of rooms. This is separated from the rooms by a void in order to reduce noise transmission, and pairs of rooms on the second floor are reached by discreet staircases.

Over the years the hotel has been subjected to regular makeovers which have raised its star ratings, increased its prices and diminished its charms.

OPPOSITE LEFT: The staircase at the south end of the main block (added in 1973).

OPPOSITE RIGHT: The curved staircase in the southern block (1973).

OPPOSITE MIDDLE AND RIGHT: The staircase at the end of the southern block (added in 1973).

The Neptune Hotel
(aka Maha Gedara)
BERUWALA, 1974

The Neptune hotel was designed with two parallel arms of rooms connected by a central reception pavilion that together create a large garden court that faces the sea. Geoffrey raised the reception area to first-floor level in order to create a more theatrical entrance. A large pond was excavated on the land side of the hotel and turned into a jungle-like water garden while the excavated material was used to lift the *porte-cochère* to first-floor level.

Visitors are treated to a dramatic entrance sequence. Having experienced the surprise encounter with the water garden, they are drawn up a curving ramp to a *porte-cochère* and, having passed through the reception, arrive in a beautiful lounge that opens on to a large terrace with views out across the garden court towards the ocean.

The terrace doubles as the roof to the dining loggia and the two levels are connected by an external pre-cast concrete spiral staircase.

LEFT: Two views of the staircase beside the main lounge.

OPPOSITE: A spiral staircase linking the upper terrace to the restaurant and pool (1973).

The State Mortgage Bank
(aka The Mahaweli Building)
UNION PLACE, COLOMBO, 1977

The State Mortgage Bank tower can be regarded as a prototype for a low-energy high-rise office building in a tropical city. It contained a bank on its ground floor with ten floors of offices and a double-height roof loggia. Its aileron-shaped plan was oriented to minimise solar intrusion and maximise ventilation and its section included special monsoon windows that incorporated ventilation baffles. The two staircases reflect the geometry of the building and are both trapezoidal in plan.

Malaysian architect Ken Yeang later hailed the tower as the world's first bio-climatic skyscraper, though it has been poorly maintained and now looks quite shabby.

OPPOSITE AND RIGHT: Views of the main stair: the geometry reflects the overall geometry of the building.

The Martenstyn House
KANNANGARA MAWATHA, COLOMBO, 1978

The Martenstyn house was built in a corner of the garden of a house that Geoffrey had built some ten years earlier. As a consequence, it was restricted to a small footprint and rose three floors to a roof terrace through the branches of a massive bo tree.

The staircase begins as a straight flight from the tunnelled entrance and then transforms into a cranked dog-leg on the upper floors. The stair flights are of white-painted pre-cast concrete with tile-inset treads while the slender handrail and supports are of black painted steel. Although the underside of the lower flight is smooth, the upper flights have stepped soffits. The cranked geometry and the minimalist construction together give the staircase a highly sculptural feel.

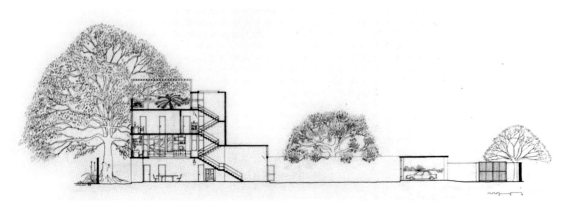

LEFT TOP: Section through the house showing the relationship of the staircase to the entrance tunnel.

BOTTOM LEFT: The straight lower flight that extends down to meet the entrance tunnel.

BOTTOM RIGHT: The first-floor landing.

OPPOSITE: A view up the stairwell. The house was recently restored by Bawa's former associate, Channa Daswatte. The hanging mobile is a new work by Bawa's long-time collaborator Laki Senanayake.

House for Lidia Duchini
(aka No 87)
GALLE ROAD, BENTOTA, 1979

When Geoffrey suggested to his friend Lidia Duchini that she buy the villa in Bentota that later became the Mohoti Walaawe, she chose instead to buy a smaller house on the east side of the main road, mainly because it offered her a large garden. Having turned the house around so that it faced away from the road and into the garden, Geoffrey persuaded her to buy a second dilapidated house that stood on the opposite side of the road and rebuilt it at right angles within the garden.

The second house needed a new staircase and for this Geoffrey designed one of his most bizarre creations at the centre of the plan. It first rises three steps to a plinth and then climbs in three flights via two square landings. The second landing is supported on a Tuscan column carved from a single piece of timber. The detailed drawings and details were executed by C Anjalendran.

LEFT: The attic gallery within the roof space.

BELOW: An original drawing of the main staircase by C Anjalendran.

OPPOSITE: The staircase twists its way up to the attic.

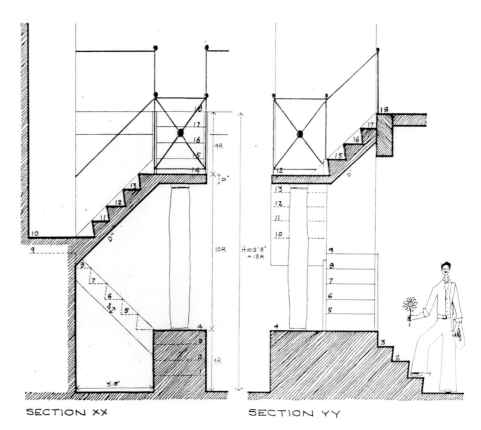

SECTION XX   SECTION YY

Mohoti Walaawe
(aka The Villa)
BENTOTA, 1979 ONWARDS

When Geoffrey discovered an old villa on the southern edge of Bentota between the main road and the railway line, he tried in vain to persuade various friends to buy it. Finally, he bought it himself and converted it into a boutique hotel, adding extra rooms in two new wings to the north. This was the first hotel of its kind in Sri Lanka. Having tried to run it himself for a few years, he later leased it and eventually sold it to professional hoteliers. More recently it has been subject to some alterations and additions, though, happily, a number of interesting staircases survive.

OPPOSITE LEFT: The restored staircase within the original house.

OPPOSITE RIGHT: The pool court.

RIGHT: The narrow stair up from the pool to a guest suite.

Institute of Integral Education
(aka Subodhi)
PILIYANDALA, 1979

The Institute for Integral Education was conceived as a study retreat for the Catholic Church on the banks of the Bolgoda Lake. The retreat was built on sloping ground within an old coconut estate and occupied opposing sides of a steep-sided valley. A library and auditorium marked the entrance and were placed on the southern flank of the valley while the dormitory blocks occupied the northern flank, the two being connected by a central hall that spanned them like a bridge.

The budget was tight and the construction had to be simple. Geoffrey added interest in the way he placed the buildings on the site and in his designs for the many staircases that were needed. Two in particular command attention: the entrance staircase than runs down the southern flank is buried in an underground tunnel, while the stairs up to the dormitories are covered by a cascade of roofs.

OPPOSITE: Stairs on the hillside below the entrance loggia.

RIGHT: The cascade of stairs on the north side of the valley.

ABOVE LEFT AND RIGHT: The covered way running down the south side of the valley. A narrow stair that connects the bridging pavilion down to the valley floor.

OPPOSITE: The underground tunnel cut into the hillside to connect the entrance to the central pavilion.

Triton Hotel
(aka Heritance Ahungalla)
AHUNGALLA, 1979

As the Triton Hotel site boasts a long waterfront, it would have been simple to line up the accommodation along the beach. But Geoffrey chose instead to break the building up into short blocks, three storeys in height, and place them at different angles in order to create open-sided garden courts and cool enclosed lightwells. This avoids the banality of the obvious and provides every room with its own unique view of the sea. The visitor approaches down a narrow, enclosed lane and is met by a cohort of coconut palms standing in a reflecting pool. The surface merges with the polished floor of the reception hall, the surface of the swimming pool and the waters of the Indian Ocean beyond. As Bawa observed: "If the world were flat you would see Africa!"

Again, every staircase is unique: that in the main lobby is decorated with murals by Laki Senanayake; another is guarded by a huge hooded cobra.

OPPOSITE LEFT: The imposing cobra stair in the south wing.

OPPOSITE RIGHT: Staircases in one of the lightwells in the north wing.

RIGHT: The main stair in the entrance lobby with murals by Laki Senanayake.

New Sri Lanka Parliament
KOTTE, 1980

When Bawa was commissioned in 1978 by President J R Jayawardene to design a new Parliament in a swamp some eight kilometres east of Colombo, he proposed draining the valley to create a lake with an island at its centre. A principal pavilion containing the main debating chamber was placed at the centre of the island and was surrounded by a cluster of asymmetrically placed satellite pavilions, all covered by hipped copper roofs.

At state openings of Parliament, the President travels by car from the Presidential Secretariat in Colombo and arrives at the foot of a broad flight of steps that leads up to the entrance arcade. From here a ceremonial staircase passes up through massive silver doors and arrives on the floor of the debating chamber. Parliamentarians watch the President as he appears head first through the floor of the House between the stepped rows of desks while members of the public look down from steeply raked tribunes under the curving metal ceiling.

Other staircases abound: the raked tribune around two sides of the public debating pavilion; the broad stair that links the members' gardens to the upper terraces; the staircase that leads to the members' dining room, are a few examples.

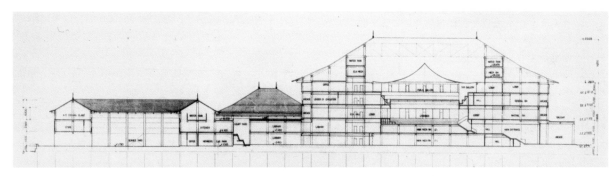

LEFT TOP: A section through the debating chamber showing the ceremonial staircase that rises from the loggia up to the floor of the chamber.

LEFT BELOW: An aerial view of the Parliament site.

OPPOSITE: A view down into the debating chamber showing the gently raked members' seating and the steeply raked visitors' gallery.

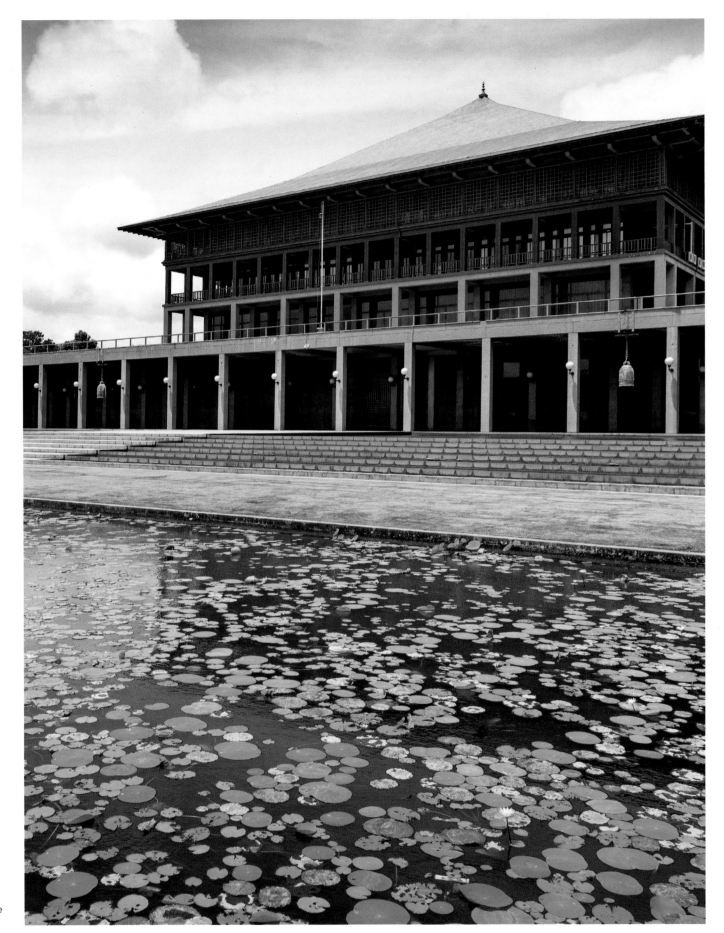

OPPOSITE TOP: The ceremonial stair that leads up to the debating chamber.

OPPOSITE BELOW: The murals on the flanking walls of the staircase are by the painter-monk Manjusri who was a member of the 43 Group.

RIGHT: The reflecting pool and stepped water rill in the entrance plaza.

Ruhunu University Campus
MATARA, 1980–85

The Ruhunu University campus was built between 1980 and 1985 and consists of around 50 different buildings with a total area of 50,000 square metres. It lies to the east of Matara on three hills that overlook the Indian Ocean. Although Geoffrey tried to build along the contours and avoid too many level changes, it contains, not surprisingly, a very large number of staircases.

Bawa was forced by budgetary constraints to use simple construction methods and a limited palette of materials. But he created variety by the way he placed buildings in relation to the site's contours and developed a strong dialogue between architecture and landscape. The buildings were designed on a planning grid of 30 metres, a structural grid of 3 metres and a vertical grid of 1.5 metres. The grids were, for the most part aligned on a north-south axis, or turned through 30° or 45° to suit the terrain.

One might have expected there to be a total uniformity of details, as was often the case in the building of new universities in Europe, but Bawa introduced variety throughout the campus. In particular he clearly derived enormous pleasure in designing the different staircases, from the monumental sequence of stairs that climbs through the administration building to the summit of the eastern hill to the tiny individual staircases that pop up throughout the arts faculty.

BELOW: An aerial view of the south-eastern hill showing the library and the main arts complex.

BELOW RIGHT: External staircases leading up to the main arts complex.

OPPOSITE: The stepped valley next to the library.

ABOVE: The interior of the library.

OPPOSITE: The main staircase on the
axis of the arts complex.

ABOVE LEFT: An intriguing staircase in the arts complex – the built-in bench beneath the half-landing is a popular meeting place for lovers.

ABOVE RIGHT:: A staircase at a meeting point of covered walkways.

OPPOSITE: A staircase in the Science Faculty.

House for Sunethra Bandaranaike
HORAGOLLA, 1985

The house for Sunethra Bandaranaike was converted from an old building that had begun as the Bandaranaike family home and then had been converted into a stable block when a new house was built to its southwest. When commissioned to renovate and redesign the stables into a country home, Bawa cocooned the main pavilion with two generous walled garden courts. The stable hall became the main sitting room and a pair of timber mezzanines were introduced to reduce its scale and provide smaller sitting spaces. The staircase up to the mezzanine rose in a series of short flights which provide a deliberately discordant element to interrupt the overall symmetry.

BELOW: The former stable block that now forms the main element of the house.

BELOW RIGHT: Stair up to the mezzanine bedroom in the guest wing.

OPPOSITE: The staircase leading up to the gallery in what was the stable hall and is now the sitting room.

Fitzherbert House
(aka Claughton)
DIKWELLA, 1986

Claughton Bungalow was built as a holiday home for a British estate agent called Richard Fitzherbert Brockholes. It sits in a grove of coconut trees on the headland that forms the western side of Kudawella Bay. A cluster of three separate courtyard suites are linked by a main loggia which contains a dining veranda on its upper level and a lounge below. The staircase that connects the two levels marks the beginning of a chain of stairs that are cut into the hillside and wind down through the garden to an outdoor pool poised far below on the edge of the cliffs.

OPPOSITE View of the house from the coconut grove.

RIGHT: The staircase links the various levels of the main pavilion before initiating the route down through the coconut grove to the pool.

ABOVE AND OPPOSITE: Two views of
the stepped pathway that descends
through the coconut grove from the
house to the pool.

Chloe de Soysa House
DHARMAPALA MAWATHA, COLOMBO, 1987

The de Soysas wanted to build a compact town house and office at the end of the garden of their family home. The result was one of a series of tower houses that Bawa built during the final decade of his practice. The building rises on four levels amongst the trees of the de Soysas' former garden. The ground floor is given over to a carport and office. The first floor contains a glass-walled sitting room that runs between two open terraces as well as a guest bedroom. The second floor is given over entirely to the main bedroom which seems to float amongst the trees. The top level carries a secluded roof garden. The three principal levels are served by an elegant dog-leg staircase, whilst the top level is reached via a straight and narrow steel flight.

BELOW: **View from the stair to the first-floor sitting room.**

OPPOSITE: **The main stair with the narrow passage to the kitchen.**

Kandalama Hotel
DAMBULLA, 1992

When Geoffrey was invited to design a hotel near to the rock citadel at Sigiriya, he rejected the site and persuaded his clients to locate their hotel some eight kilometres away to the south on a cliff overlooking the ancient Kandalama reservoir which also gave a distant view of the citadel.

The hotel was built on six levels and wrapped itself in a kilometre-long snake around the cliff. It was conceived like some giant ocean liner, with decks above and cabins below, that has come aground on a remote mountainside. Its rugged architecture was reminiscent of an ancient palace and it functioned as a belvedere, a place from which to admire the views of the reservoir and the surrounding jungle.

Inevitably, it is laced with staircases: wide steps greet the visitor and lead up through a cave to the main reception lounge; a staircase of angled flights is guarded by a massive bronze owl by Laki Senanayake; an elegant square stair links the main reception to the upper lounges.

ABOVE: **A section through the hotel showing the relationship between the main residential block and the cliff.**

LEFT: **The hotel entrance.**

OPPOSITE: **The entrance by night.**

LEFT TOP: The north elevation with rooms looking over the reservoir towards Sigiriya.

LEFT BELOW: The staircase in the knuckle of the Sigiriya Wing.

OPPOSITE TOP: A sculpted owl by Laki Senanayake swoops over the main staircase linking the reception level to the dining room.

OPPOSITE BELOW LEFT: The staircase in the knuckle of the Sigiriya Wing.

OPPOSITE BELOW RIGHT: The formal staircase linking the main lounges.

Jayakody House
PARK STREET, COLOMBO, 1992

Geoffrey designed this magical house on a small, awkwardly shaped plot of land in the centre of the city for flower entrepreneur Rohan Jayakody. The house comprised accommodation on three floors, as well as an upper roof terrace with a swimming pool. The lower floor was moulded to fit the site and was lit by small 'left-over' courts and lightwells. The upper floors were progressively reduced in area to make way for courtyards and terraces.

The house contains an interesting collection of staircases. A main dog-leg staircase and, behind it, a narrow service staircase, connect the ground floor entrance with the two bedroom floors. A straight staircase climbs up within a rear courtyard to the roof terraces. The elegant second-floor terrace is connected up to the pool terrace by a spiral staircase contained within a steel tower in the manner of a bird-cage — an echo of the vertiginous stairs that give access to the cliff-face murals at Sigiriya.

OPPOSITE LEFT: A view across the second-floor terrace towards the birdcage staircase that connects to the upper roof terrace.

OPPOSITE MIDDLE: The foot of the birdcage staircase.

OPPOSITE RIGHT: The main stair within the house.

RIGHT: Stair from the second floor courtyard up to the roof terrace.

Lighthouse Hotel
GALLE, 1995–97

The Lighthouse Hotel was built on a rocky headland to the north of Galle and takes the full brunt of the southwest monsoon. In the main reception building a circular staircase, contained within a generous circular drum, winds its way up from the ground-floor *porte-cochère* to the main floor and thence to an upper pool court. The staircase was designed by Geoffrey's artist friend Laki Senanayake and was conceived as a swirling mass of warriors, formed of beaten metal, who re-enact the 17th-century battle of Randeniya fought between the Sinhalese and the Portuguese. In a reference to Galle's Arab connections, the drum is capped by a shallow dome which has a circular opening or oculus at its centre. This produces a shaft of light that tracks around the wall of the drum as the day progresses, and is reminiscent of the oculus in the dome of the Pantheon in Rome.

The main floor opens on to stepped terraces which connect down via rugged stone staircases to the edge of the ocean, recalling the stairs and terraces on the summit of Sigiriya.

Beyond the reception building, two cranked accommodation blocks slide past each other to create an enclosed courtyard and an open pool court. The blocks are served by a number of staircases, each of them a response to the unique geometry of their situation. The pool court is connected down to waterside lawns by a succession of ramps and stairs inspired by Baroque garden architecture.

OPPOSITE AND RIGHT: The main staircase with Laki Senanayake's sculpted balusters depicting the 17th-century battle of Radeniya fought between the Kandyans and the Portuguese.

OPPOSITE TOP: External stair on the side of the east wing.

OPPOSITE BELOW: Stairs in the link between the east and west wings.

RIGHT TOP: The north end of the east wing with the ramps and stairs that link the upper and lower gardens.

RIGHT BELOW: Close-up of the ramps and stairs.

LEFT: Water cascade below the swimming pool.

OPPOSITE: Stairs in the knuckle of the west wing.

Blue Water Hotel
WADDUWA, 1997

The Blue Water Hotel is situated to the immediate south of Colombo in a coconut grove that lies between the railway and the Indian Ocean. Its Palladian formality creates the aura of a suburban palazzo. An axial arcade connects the *porte-cochère* across a large grassy court to the main buildings which are split into linked blocks of three and four storeys that face the sea through the serried ranks of coconut trees. These are served by a number of elegant staircases.

OPPOSITE: Two views of the main stair that rises up from the reception area.

RIGHT: The junction of the long entrance mall with the residential block is marked by a series of stepped water features.

OVERLEAF: Three views of the square staircase that connects the main transverse mall with the lateral corridors that serve the rooms.

The David Spenser House
ROSMEAD PLACE, COLOMBO, 1997

David Spenser was born in Colombo but made his name first as a child actor on British television and then as a theatre and film producer. His house, one of Bawa's last, was built on a small plot at the end of a lane off Rosmead Place. Conceived as a tower, its three main floors are served by a dog-leg stair, while an open steel stair connects up to the rooftop swimming pool.

OPPOSITE: Two views of the main staircase. The house was built for an elderly couple and the stair was designed with shallow risers and wide treads.

RIGHT: The staircase up to the secret pool terrace on the roof.

The Jayawardene House
MIRISSA, 1997

The Jayawardene House was the last that Bawa completed before he suffered a stroke in 1998. Perched high on the Red Cliffs overlooking Weligama Bay, it was designed as a weekend house. A simple low-pitched roof is supported on 21 slender concrete-enclosed steel columns and seems to float in the surrounding grove of casuarina trees. Beneath it is a vast open veranda that forms the principle living space. One end of this steps up to create a raised platform that acts as a sitting and sleeping deck and forms the roof of a lower basement area. The basement contains two small sleeping cells and a bathroom and opens into a small courtyard at the edge of the cliff. The staircase which connects the loggia to the basement is located at the centre of the plan and is enclosed within a glass-sided prism.

OPPOSITE TOP: A section through the cliff, showing the way in which one end of the open loggia steps up as a mezzanine above a sunken bedroom floor.

OPPOSITE BELOW LEFT: The silhouette of the cliff.

OPPOSITE BELOW RIGHT: The open loggia.

RIGHT TOP: A view across the loggia with the raised mezzanine on the right, showing how the staircase down to the bedrooms is contained within a glass aedicule.

RIGHT MIDDLE: The staircase with its vertically pivoted doors closed.

RIGHT BOTTOM: The raised mezzanine, used as a sitting room or an open sleeping area.

PAGE 176: An owl by Laki Senanayake swoops over the main staircase linking the reception level to the dining room at the Kandalama Hotel.

Glossary

dagaba a solid masonry hemisphere built around a closed relic chamber, found in Buddhist temples (also known as a *stupa*)

dog-leg (staircase) a staircase comprising two opposing half-flights of stairs connected by a half-landing

going (staircase) the horizontal net depth of a staircase tread

moonstone a sculpted semi-circle of stone acting as a threshold at the foot of a traditional Buddhist staircase

piano nobile the main floor of a classical building

pitch (staircase) the angle of staircase expressed either as the ratio of the rise to the going or as an angle

porte-cochère a covered entrance (literally the coach porch)

rise (staircase) the vertical height of a staircase tread

spiral (staircase) a circular staircase with tapered treads

vatadage a roofed *dagaba*

winder a tapering staircase tread

Bibliography

Anjalendran, C, David Robson and Dominic Sansoni. *The Architectural Heritage of Sri Lanka*. Singapore: Talisman, 2015.

Bawa, Geoffrey. *Balthasar Neumann and His Architecture*. unpublished dissertation presented to the Architectural Association, London, 1957.

Bawa, Geoffrey, Christoph Bon and Dominic Sansoni. *Lunuganga*. Singapore: Times Editions, 1990.

Lewcock, Ronald, Barbara Sansoni and Laki Senanayake. *The Architecture of an Island*. Colombo: Barefoot, 1998.

Robson David. *Bawa: The Complete Works*. London: Thames and Hudson, 2002.

Robson David. *Beyond Bawa*. London: Thames and Hudson, 2007.

Robson David and Dominic Sansoni. *Bawa: The Sri Lanka Gardens*. London: Thames and Hudson, 2008.

Robson David and Sebastian Posingis. *In Search of Bawa*. Singapore: Talisman, 2016.

Sansoni, Dominic, Sebastian Posingis and Richard Simon. *Sri Lanka: The Island from Above*. Colombo: Sansoni Warehouse, 2017.

Sitwell, Sir George. *On the Making of Gardens*. London: John Murray, 1909.

Photo Credits

All photographs by Sebastian Posingis. With the following exceptions:

Banuka Vithanage. Page 116

Bayerische Schlösserverwaltung, Maria Scherf, München. Page 43

Bayerische Schlösserverwaltung, Ulrich Pfeuffer, München. Pages 40

Boris Breytman. Page 45

Courtesy of C Anjelandran. Pages 110, 126

Courtesy of Rolf Winkler. Page 24 (middle)

Dominic Sansoni. Pages 50 (left and middle), 51 (right), 54 (left), 56, 57, 58 (left)

David Robson. Pages 12 (middle), 13 (left), 24 (right), 41 (left), 44, 68, 69, 92 (bottom left and right), 95, 115, 117, 173

David Robson Archive. Pages 14 (left, middle and right), 15 (left and right), 16, 50 (right), 78 (drawing), 79 (drawing), 90 (top left and bottom left), 92, 94 (plan and section), 95 (top right), 96, 106 (section), 113 (top), 114, 124 (drawing), 136, 154, 172

Federico Zeri Foundation. Page 22, this photographic reproduction was provided by the Photo Archive of the Federico Zeri Foundation. The property rights of the author have been met.

Luxshmanan Nadaraja. Pages 66, 67

Produced with permission of the Art Gallery of New South Wales and the Estate of Donald Friend (gift of Mrs Varcoe). Page 13 (right)

W L H Skeen, (1874–1903), English photographer, Sansoni Collection. Page 55

Wikimedia Commons, Daryl Mitchell. Page 25

Wikimedia Commons, I, Saiko. Page 13 (middle)

Wikimedia Commons, public domains. Pages 12 (right), 41 (right), 42

Acknowledgments

The author and photographer have spent many years living in and travelling around Sri Lanka and are indebted to the advice and help they have received from their numerous Sri Lankan friends and acquaintances, among them, most especially, the photographer Dominic Sansoni and the architect C Anjalendran. They would like to acknowledge the help and support that they have received from the Geoffrey Bawa Trust and its manager Priyanka Tisseveerasinghe. Finally, they would also like to thank their respective partners, Ursula Robson and Line Rindebaek for their patient support.